RETIRE FEARLESSLY

Unveiling the 50+ Financial Security Code

TROY CHAMBERS

Table of Contents

Preface

Picture this: You wake up on a crisp morning, not to the blaring sound of an alarm clock, but to the gentle caress of sunlight filtering through your curtains. You savor a leisurely breakfast, knowing that the day is yours to explore, create, and relish.

No more deadlines, no more rush-hour traffic, and no more workplace stress. Welcome to the world of "Retire Fearlessly: Unveiling the 50+ Financial Security Code" - where your dream retirement becomes an exhilarating reality.

Hey there, future retirees and adventure-seekers! If you're ready to embark on a journey that will redefine your notion of retirement, then fasten your seatbelts, because we're about to take off on a thrilling ride. I'm your co-pilot, and my mission is simple: to guide you toward a retirement that's not only financially secure but also brimming with excitement and endless possibilities.

Retirement planning sounds like a snooze-fest, you might be thinking. But fear not, my friend, because this is not your typical retirement guide. This book is your ticket to an extraordinary chapter of your life - a chapter filled with laughter, exploration, and the freedom to live life on your terms.

So, let me ask you something: Have you ever daydreamed about post-retirement adventures? Maybe you've imagined embarking on an exotic travel spree, taking up a passion project, or simply spending quality time with loved ones.

Well, here's the secret sauce: all those dreams can come true with a little bit of planning and a sprinkle of fearlessness.

Whether you're on the cusp of retirement or have already entered this new phase, you're in the right place. We'll debunk the myths, address the fears, and empower you with the knowledge to tackle retirement head-on, without hesitation.

But hey, let's get real for a moment - we know life isn't all rainbows and unicorns. Retirement can be daunting, and financial decisions can feel like navigating a maze. That's why we've got your back! We'll demystify the complexities, making sure you have the tools and insights to make smart choices that align with your goals and values.

And guess what? Retirement isn't just about kicking back and relaxing (although there's plenty of that too!). It's about discovering new passions, finding purpose, and positively impacting the world around you. In these pages, we'll dive into the art of crafting a retirement that nourishes your soul and fuels your sense of adventure.

From tackling your finances like a pro to embracing technology that makes life easier, we've got a buffet of tips and strategies to satisfy your retirement appetite. And the best part? It's all served with a friendly, down-to-earth attitude that will leave you feeling empowered and excited about your future.

So, if you're ready to trade the daily grind for a life of fulfillment and financial security, turn the page, and let's start scripting the tale of your fearless retirement. Get ready to seize the day, unleash your passions, and embark on a journey that will redefine what it means to be 50+ and fabulous!

Buckle up, my friend - we're about to make your retirement dreams take flight!

Introduction

The Changing Landscape of Retirement Planning for 50+

Welcome to the dawn of a new era in retirement planning! As we delve into the world of "Retire Fearlessly: Unveiling the 50+ Financial Security Code," it's essential to grasp the seismic shifts transforming the retirement landscape for the 50+ generation. Gone are the days of traditional retirement norms; we now find ourselves at the crossroads of longevity, ambition, and self-reliance.

Demographic Shifts and Increased Life Expectancy

Let's kick off our journey by acknowledging a fundamental game-changer: demographic shifts and increased life expectancy. In the past century, remarkable advancements in healthcare, technology, and overall living standards have led to longer, healthier lives. A longer life expectancy means that retirement isn't just a brief pause before the final chapter; it's a vibrant and extended phase to be celebrated.

Imagine Jane, who's 55 and retiring in this dynamic era. She's not thinking about retirement as the end; instead, she sees it as a new beginning, a chance to explore her passions and pursue those dreams she postponed while building her career. With an expected lifespan of another 30 or more years, Jane's retirement planning must accommodate a fulfilling and active life ahead.

The Rise of Self-Reliance in Retirement

With this extended retirement timeline, the concept of self-reliance takes center stage. Unlike previous generations who heavily relied on employer pensions and social support, many of today's 50+ individuals face a different reality. Corporations are transitioning away from traditional pension plans, putting more responsibility on employees to secure their financial futures.

Meet John, a 60-year-old who enjoyed a successful career but realized that his retirement savings would need to do the heavy lifting. He understands the importance of taking control of his financial destiny and actively participates in planning for his retirement. John is an avid learner, seeking guidance from financial experts, and harnessing the power of digital tools to manage his investments effectively.

Embracing the Fearless Mindset for a Fulfilling Retirement

In this new landscape, embracing a fearless mindset becomes paramount. Retirement planning shouldn't be a source of dread or anxiety; it should be an exciting opportunity to design the life you've always desired. Alongside John and Jane, countless retirees have transformed their perspectives, choosing to tackle retirement with vigor and positivity.

Consider Maria, a 62-year-old retiree who was initially hesitant about the uncertainties of post-career life. Yet, she decided to face her fears head-on. Maria began by challenging herself to try new activities and rediscover old hobbies. Through networking with other retirees, she joined a local gardening club, indulging in her passion for nurturing plants and creating beautiful landscapes. Embracing a fearless mindset allowed Maria to unlock hidden talents and embark on a fulfilling journey.

Overcoming Common Retirement Fears and Concerns

Of course, embracing a fearless mindset doesn't mean challenges or concerns won't exist. Retirement comes with its fair share of worries, such as financial stability, healthcare expenses, and staying socially connected. But here's the silver lining - every concern is an opportunity for proactive planning and problem-solving.

Take Robert, a 58-year-old who was anxious about the rising costs of healthcare in retirement. He addressed this concern by diligently researching different health insurance options, exploring Medicare supplements, and planning for potential long-term care needs. Robert's preparation not only alleviated his worries but also gave him peace of mind, knowing he was ready to face any healthcare challenges that might arise.

Understanding the Power of Positive Retirement Planning

As we venture deeper into this book, the power of positive retirement planning will become your guiding light. Positive retirement planning goes beyond just crunching numbers; it involves envisioning a future filled with purpose, joy, and personal growth. By harnessing the energy of positivity, you can navigate the twists and turns of retirement with grace and determination.

Meet Michael, a 56-year-old who approached retirement planning with a positive mindset. Instead of focusing solely on finances, Michael envisioned the kind of life he wanted to lead after retiring from his demanding job. He saw retirement as an opportunity to reconnect with family and friends, mentor younger generations, and explore his artistic passions. Michael discovered a renewed sense of purpose and fulfillment through positive retirement planning.

So, are you prepared to start your transformational journey? Over the next chapters, we'll delve into the nuts and bolts of retirement planning, from evaluating your financial landscape to crafting a personalized roadmap that aligns with your dreams and aspirations.

It's time to embrace the changing tides of retirement, seize the potential of self-reliance, and ignite the fearless spirit within you.

Turn the page, and let's dive headfirst into a retirement that's not just about financial security, but a life bursting with passion, purpose, and endless possibilities. Together, we'll unleash the 50+ financial security code and set you on a path to retire fearlessly!

Chapter 1

Assessing Your Financial Readiness

Congratulations on taking the first step toward your fearless retirement journey! In this chapter, we'll dive into the crucial process of assessing your financial readiness for retirement. It's time to put on your financial detective hat and uncover the full picture of your current financial landscape. By the end of this chapter, you'll have a clear understanding of where you stand financially and be well-equipped to set achievable retirement goals.

Taking an Overall View of Your Current Financial Situation

Before we start planning for the future, we need to take a comprehensive look at where you stand today. This means evaluating your assets, savings, investments, and debts - everything that contributes to your financial well-being. Remember, a holistic view provides a realistic foundation for your retirement plan.

Evaluating Assets, Savings, and Investments

Now that we've embarked on the journey of assessing your financial readiness for retirement, let's take a closer look at evaluating your assets, savings, and investments. This critical step will help you gain a comprehensive understanding of your current financial standing and lay the groundwork for building a robust retirement plan.

Identifying Your Assets

Assets are the bedrock of your financial foundation. They encompass all your valuable possessions and resources that hold monetary value. When evaluating your assets, consider both tangible and intangible assets.

Tangible assets include your primary residence, any other real estate properties you own (e.g., vacation homes, rental properties), vehicles, valuable collections (e.g., artwork, antiques), and personal belongings. Intangible assets encompass financial assets such as cash, savings accounts, investment portfolios, retirement accounts (e.g., 401(k)s, IRAs), and other financial instruments.

Take the example of Mark and Susan, a couple in their late 50s planning for retirement. They compiled a list of their assets, which included their home, a rental property generating rental income, a diverse investment portfolio comprising stocks and bonds, and a sizeable retirement account they had been diligently contributing over the years. By identifying their assets, Mark and Susan gained a clear sense of their current financial strength and potential sources of income during retirement.

Understanding Your Savings

Savings are the reservoir of financial security you've been nurturing over time. Your savings play a crucial role in providing a safety net during retirement and funding your future goals and dreams.

Evaluate your savings accounts, including checking accounts, savings accounts, and certificates of deposit (CDs). Additionally, assess any liquid assets that can be easily accessed for emergencies or unforeseen expenses.

Liquid assets may include money market funds or other short-term investments that you can quickly convert to cash when needed.

Meet Laura, a single professional in her early 60s preparing for retirement. She meticulously reviewed her savings accounts, which included an emergency fund with three to six months' worth of living expenses, a high-yield savings account, and a money market fund. Having a well-established emergency fund and liquid savings provided Laura with a sense of financial security and peace of mind as she approached retirement.

Analyzing Your Investments

Investments can be powerful tools for wealth accumulation and long-term financial growth. As you assess your investments, consider their performance, diversification, and alignment with your risk tolerance and retirement goals.

Review your investment portfolio to ensure it is diversified across various asset classes, industries, and geographic regions. Diversification can help mitigate risks and optimize potential returns. Additionally, examine the performance of individual investments and evaluate whether they align with your risk appetite and time horizon.

For example, John, a 59-year-old investor, analyzed his investment portfolio, which included a mix of stocks, bonds, and mutual funds. He noticed that some individual stocks were highly volatile and didn't align with his risk tolerance as he neared retirement. John decided to rebalance his portfolio to reduce risk and enhance stability, ensuring his investments were better suited for his retirement goals.

In conclusion, evaluating your assets, savings, and investments is an essential step in the process of assessing your financial readiness for retirement. By understanding your assets, including tangible and intangible resources, you gain a holistic view of your financial strength.

Analyzing your savings provides a safety net and the means to handle emergencies while evaluating your investments helps optimize growth and align your portfolio with your retirement goals.

Calculating Liabilities, Debts, and Monthly Expenses

In our pursuit of fearless retirement planning, it's time to dive deeper into the financial ocean and examine the crucial aspects of liabilities, debts, and monthly expenses. Understanding these key components is essential for building a solid retirement plan that addresses potential financial challenges and ensures a smooth transition into retirement.

Assessing Your Liabilities

Liabilities encompass all the financial obligations and debts you owe. As we assess your liabilities, it's essential to identify both short-term and long-term financial commitments.

Short-term liabilities may include credit card balances, personal loans, and any outstanding bills that require immediate attention. Long-term liabilities typically consist of your mortgage and any other loans with extended repayment periods.

Consider the example of Alex, a 55-year-old individual who decided to assess his liabilities before planning for retirement. He discovered that his short-term liabilities included credit card debt accumulated during a recent home renovation project. Additionally, Alex identified his mortgage as a significant long-term liability. By understanding his liabilities, Alex could prioritize debt repayment and plan for a debt-free retirement.

Tackling Your Debts

Debt management is a crucial aspect of fearless retirement planning. As you approach retirement, minimizing or eliminating debts can significantly impact your financial security and provide more flexibility in your retirement budget.

Start by reviewing your outstanding debts and their corresponding interest rates. High-interest debts, such as credit card balances, can hinder your financial progress and eat into your retirement savings. Focus on paying off high-interest debts first while continuing to make minimum payments on other debts.

Continuing with Alex's example, he decided to create a debt repayment strategy. He prioritized paying off his high-interest credit card debt while maintaining regular payments on his mortgage and other loans. With a clear plan in place, Alex began chipping away at his debts, bringing him one step closer to a debt-free retirement.

Analyzing Your Monthly Expenses

Understanding your monthly expenses is vital for estimating the funds needed to maintain your desired lifestyle during retirement. As you assess your expenses, consider both essential and discretionary spending categories.

Essential expenses encompass the costs necessary for maintaining your daily living, such as housing, utilities, groceries, insurance premiums, transportation, and healthcare. Discretionary expenses, on the other hand, include non-essential spending on entertainment, dining out, vacations, hobbies, and other lifestyle choices.

Meet Lisa, a 60-year-old individual keen on calculating her monthly expenses for retirement planning. By tracking her expenses, Lisa realized that dining out and entertainment expenses accounted for a significant portion of her discretionary spending. As she prepared for retirement, Lisa made conscious adjustments to her budget, allocating more funds towards her travel aspirations and reducing expenses on non-essential items.

Calculating your liabilities, debts, and monthly expenses is a pivotal step in assessing your financial readiness for retirement. By gaining insight into your financial obligations, you can develop strategies to manage and eliminate debts, ensuring a smoother financial journey into retirement.

Determining Your Retirement Goals and Lifestyle Expectations

As we delve deeper into the realms of fearless retirement planning, it's time to shift our focus toward envisioning your retirement goals and lifestyle expectations. Retirement isn't just a finish line; it's an opportunity to create a life that aligns with your aspirations, passions, and dreams. By identifying your retirement vision, you'll gain clarity on the path you want to pursue and set the stage for a truly fulfilling retirement experience.

Identifying Your Retirement Vision and Dreams

Welcome to the exhilarating phase of fearless retirement planning - identifying your retirement vision and dreams. Retirement isn't just a distant event; it's an opportunity to create a life that aligns with your passions, values, and deepest desires. By delving into your aspirations and envisioning your ideal retirement, you'll unlock a sense of purpose and excitement that will guide your financial decisions and shape the path to a truly fulfilling retirement experience.

Visualizing Your Ideal Retirement

Close your eyes for a moment and let your imagination soar. Picture your perfect retirement - what does it look like? This is your canvas to paint the life you've always envisioned, free from the constraints of a 9-to-5 routine. Your retirement dreams are as unique as you are, and this is the time to explore and embrace them.

Consider the activities and experiences that bring you joy and fulfillment. Are you drawn to traveling the world, immersing yourself in new cultures and breathtaking landscapes? Or does your heart yearn to spend quality time with family and friends, creating cherished memories together? Maybe your dream retirement involves pursuing long-neglected passions, starting a new venture, or giving back to the community through volunteer work.

Let's delve into the story of William, a 62-year-old individual who always dreamt of retiring to a peaceful coastal town. William envisioned spending his days walking along the beach, savoring the ocean breeze, and immersing himself in nature's wonders. By visualizing his ideal retirement, William felt a renewed sense of purpose and fulfillment, igniting the spark to turn his dream into reality.

Identifying Your Core Passions and Interests

Retirement opens the door to a new chapter of life, providing the opportunity to explore passions and interests that may have taken a backseat during your working years. Take this time to identify your core passions and interests - the things that make your heart race and your soul come alive.

Reflect on the activities that fill you with enthusiasm and excitement. Do you have a creative flair for painting, writing, or playing a musical instrument? Are you passionate about gardening, photography, cooking, or woodworking?

Consider the hobbies that bring you a deep sense of contentment and consider how you can incorporate them into your retirement vision.

Meet Susan, a 58-year-old retiree who rediscovered her love for gardening during retirement planning. Susan recalled how nurturing plants and creating beautiful landscapes had brought her immense joy in her youth. She decided to incorporate gardening as a central element of her retirement vision, envisioning a garden filled with vibrant blooms and a serene oasis to unwind. By identifying her core passion for gardening, Susan was well on her way to designing a retirement that resonated with her soul.

Embracing Purposeful Activities and Giving Back

Retirement offers a chance to find renewed purpose and meaning through activities that enrich your life and the lives of others. Consider how you can make a positive impact in your community or pursue endeavors that contribute to a cause you deeply care about.

Think about volunteering opportunities that align with your passions or skills. Whether it's mentoring young minds, supporting environmental conservation efforts, or contributing to humanitarian causes, giving back can be a source of immense fulfillment during retirement.

For instance, let's explore the journey of Daniel, a 65-year-old retiree who had a keen interest in education. Daniel envisioned teaching computer skills to underprivileged children in his neighborhood. By embracing this purposeful activity, Daniel found a sense of fulfillment and pride in sharing his knowledge and empowering the next generation. Engaging in such activities can infuse your retirement with a profound sense of purpose and fulfillment.

Identifying your retirement vision and dreams is a pivotal step in fearless retirement planning. By visualizing your ideal retirement and exploring your passions, you'll discover a wellspring of inspiration that will guide your financial decisions and shape your retirement plan.

Embracing purposeful activities and giving back to the community will add depth and fulfillment to your retirement years, allowing you to create a life that celebrates your core values and resonates with your soul.

Setting Realistic Financial Milestones for Retirement

Welcome to the transformative phase of fearless retirement planning, where we delve into setting realistic financial milestones to turn your retirement dreams into achievable targets. Retirement planning is not just about hoping for the best; it's about creating a solid financial roadmap that aligns with your goals and aspirations.

By setting well-defined milestones, you'll gain a clear understanding of your financial needs and be empowered to take confident steps toward a secure and fulfilling retirement.

Determining Your Retirement Age and Life Expectancy

The first step in setting realistic financial milestones is determining the age at which you plan to retire. Consider factors such as your current age, your desired lifestyle during retirement, and your health status. While some individuals may wish to retire early, others might choose to work longer to enhance their financial security.

It's crucial to estimate your life expectancy based on your family history, lifestyle choices, and overall health. Remember, retirement can span several decades, and planning for a longer life ensures you have the necessary funds to support yourself throughout your retirement journey.

For example, let's follow the story of Matthew, a 55-year-old professional who aspired to retire at 65. He carefully evaluated his health status and family history to estimate his life expectancy. Matthew realized that his parents had lived well into their 90s, and he decided to plan for a retirement that could potentially span three decades. This insight influenced his approach to setting financial milestones that would sustain him through a lengthy retirement.

Estimating Your Retirement Lifestyle Expenses

Once you've determined your retirement age and life expectancy, it's time to estimate your retirement lifestyle expenses. Consider the type of lifestyle you desire during retirement and the corresponding costs. This includes housing preferences (e.g., downsizing or maintaining multiple properties), healthcare needs, travel plans, leisure activities, and any other significant expenses.

Review your current spending patterns and project how they might change during retirement. While some expenses may decrease, others, such as travel or healthcare costs, may increase. Inflation factor to ensure your retirement funds retain their purchasing power in the future.

Take the example of Olivia, a 60-year-old individual envisioning a retirement filled with travel and exploration. She meticulously analyzed her travel plans and estimated the costs associated with her desired destinations and experiences. Olivia also factored in potential healthcare expenses and leisure activities she planned to pursue during retirement. By estimating her retirement lifestyle expenses, Olivia could set financial milestones that aligned with her dreams and aspirations.

Building a Retirement Budget

With a clear picture of your retirement lifestyle expenses, it's time to build a comprehensive retirement budget. Your budget will serve as a roadmap, outlining your expected income and expenses during retirement.

Start by assessing your potential sources of retirement income, such as Social Security benefits, pensions, retirement account distributions, and any other streams of income. Next, deduct your estimated expenses to determine if there is a surplus or a deficit in your budget.

For instance, let's consider the case of Richard, a 58-year-old who aimed to retire at 65. He calculated his expected Social Security benefits, and projected income from his retirement accounts, and estimated his pension payouts. Richard then subtracted his estimated retirement lifestyle expenses from his total income to gauge the financial feasibility of his retirement plan. By building a retirement budget, Richard could identify any potential gaps and make adjustments to achieve a financially secure retirement.

Accounting for Inflation and Market Volatility

Inflation and market volatility are two critical factors that can significantly impact your retirement finances. Over time, the purchasing power of money decreases due to inflation, meaning that the same amount of money will buy fewer goods and services in the future. Additionally, market fluctuations can affect the performance of your investments and retirement accounts.

When setting financial milestones, it's essential to account for these factors to ensure that your retirement funds can withstand the test of time. Consider diversifying your investment portfolio to mitigate market risks and incorporating inflation-adjusted projections into your retirement plan.

Let's follow the journey of Emma and David, a couple in their mid-50s, who planned to retire in 10 years. They decided to adjust their financial milestones to account for an average annual inflation rate and potential market volatility. Emma and David diversified their investment portfolio, allocating a portion to low-risk investments to safeguard against market fluctuations. By considering these factors, they aimed to create a retirement plan that would remain resilient in the face of economic changes.

Monitoring and Adjusting Your Milestones

Setting financial milestones is not a one-time task; it's an ongoing process. Life is dynamic, and your financial circumstances may change over time. Regularly monitor your progress towards your milestones and be prepared to make adjustments as needed.

Consider factors such as changes in your income, expenses, or family situation. Unexpected events, such as medical emergencies or changes in market conditions, may also warrant modifications to your financial milestones.

For example, let's revisit Matthew's journey. As he moved closer to retirement, he experienced a significant increase in his healthcare expenses due to unexpected medical treatments. Matthew adjusted his financial milestones to accommodate these new expenses and ensure his retirement plan remained on track.

In conclusion, setting realistic financial milestones is a critical pillar of fearless retirement planning. By determining your retirement age and life expectancy, estimating your retirement lifestyle expenses, building a comprehensive retirement budget, accounting for inflation and market volatility, and monitoring and adjusting your milestones, you'll pave the way to a secure and fulfilling retirement.

Chapter 2

Creating a Comprehensive Retirement Plan

Congratulations on reaching Chapter 2 of your fearless retirement planning journey - creating a comprehensive retirement plan! In this chapter, we'll lay the groundwork for a robust retirement strategy that aligns with your goals and aspirations.

Building a well-defined retirement plan is like constructing a strong and stable structure - it requires careful consideration, thoughtful design, and a strategic approach to ensure it withstands the test of time.

Building the Foundation: Setting a Retirement Timeline

Assessing the Ideal Retirement Age and Phased Retirement

Determining the ideal retirement age is a crucial step in creating a comprehensive retirement plan. Your retirement age sets the stage for the rest of your life, influencing your financial security, lifestyle choices, and overall well-being during your golden years.

Let's explore the multifaceted aspects of assessing the ideal retirement age and the option of phased retirement, allowing you to make informed decisions that align with your unique circumstances and aspirations.

Factors to Consider in Assessing the Ideal Retirement Age

Financial Readiness: One of the primary considerations in determining your retirement age is your financial readiness. Evaluate your current savings, investments, and retirement accounts. Project how your savings will grow over time, taking into account contributions and potential investment returns. Consider whether your retirement funds will be sufficient to sustain your desired lifestyle during retirement.

Lifestyle Aspirations: Your envisioned lifestyle during retirement is another vital factor to consider. Do you see yourself enjoying leisurely days filled with travel and exploration? Or would you prefer a more relaxed pace, dedicating time to hobbies, family, and community engagement? Your lifestyle aspirations will influence your financial needs during retirement.

Health and Well-being: Your physical and mental health plays a significant role in determining your retirement age. Assess your current health status and any potential health concerns that may impact your ability to work or engage in desired activities during retirement. Consider the potential need for healthcare and long-term care as you age.

Life Expectancy: Estimating your life expectancy is essential for making informed decisions about your retirement age. While no one can predict the future, considering factors such as family history, lifestyle choices, and advancements in healthcare can provide insights into potential longevity.

Social Security and Pension Benefits: Evaluate the timing of your Social Security and pension benefits. Delaying Social Security benefits beyond the full retirement age can result in higher monthly payments, providing an additional source of income during retirement.

Debt and Financial Obligations: Take stock of your outstanding debts and financial obligations. Paying off high-interest debts before retiring can alleviate financial stress and allow you to allocate more resources to your retirement savings.

Exploring Phased Retirement

Phased retirement offers an alternative approach to the traditional concept of retiring at a fixed age. With phased retirement, individuals have the opportunity to gradually reduce their work hours or transition to part-time work before fully retiring. This option presents several advantages, enabling you to achieve a smoother transition into retirement and maintain a source of income during the process.

Financial Flexibility: Phased retirement allows you to maintain a steady income stream while also enjoying more leisure time. This financial flexibility can be particularly valuable if you need additional time to build your retirement savings or explore post-retirement pursuits without fully leaving the workforce.

Social Engagement: For many individuals, work provides social connections and a sense of purpose. Phased retirement allows you to continue engaging with colleagues and contributing your expertise while gradually easing into a less demanding work schedule.

Health Insurance Coverage: Access to employer-sponsored health insurance can be vital for individuals approaching retirement age. By transitioning to part-time work, you may continue to receive health insurance benefits until you are eligible for Medicare.

Testing Retirement Lifestyle: Phased retirement serves as a trial period for your retirement lifestyle. You can gauge how well your financial plan aligns with your desired lifestyle and make adjustments as needed before fully retiring.

Opportunities for Skill Development: Phased retirement offers opportunities for skill development or exploring new career paths. You can use this time to pursue interests or passions that may not have been feasible during full-time employment.

Making an Informed Decision:

As you assess the ideal retirement age and consider phased retirement, it's crucial to make an informed decision that reflects your unique circumstances and aspirations. Engage in open discussions with your financial advisor, family members, and trusted friends to gain valuable insights and perspectives.

Remember that there is no one-size-fits-all approach to retirement planning. Each individual's journey is unique, and it's essential to align your retirement age and retirement plan with your personal goals and values.

Taking the time to evaluate your financial readiness, lifestyle aspirations, health considerations, and potential benefits of phased retirement will empower you to embark on a retirement journey that brings you joy, fulfillment, and financial security.

Balancing Short-Term Needs with Long-Term Security:

In the journey of fearless retirement planning, striking the delicate balance between addressing short-term financial needs and ensuring long-term security is paramount. As you create a comprehensive retirement plan, it's essential to consider the present challenges and opportunities while safeguarding your financial well-being for the future.

Let's delve deeper into the multifaceted aspects of balancing short-term needs with long-term security to ensure that your retirement is built on a strong and resilient foundation.

Understanding Short-Term Financial Needs

Housing and Daily Living Expenses: Addressing your short-term financial needs begins with covering essential expenses such as housing, utilities, groceries, and transportation. These everyday costs form the backbone of your budget and require careful attention to ensure financial stability in the present.

Healthcare and Insurance: Healthcare is a critical consideration at any stage of life, and it becomes even more significant as you approach retirement. Ensuring adequate health insurance coverage and budgeting for healthcare expenses are essential to protect your financial well-being, especially in times of unexpected medical emergencies.

Emergency Fund: Building and maintaining an emergency fund is a vital component of addressing short-term needs. An emergency fund provides a financial safety net to cover unforeseen expenses, such as car repairs, home maintenance, or sudden unemployment, without depleting your retirement savings.

Debt Management: Paying off high-interest debts is crucial to achieving short-term financial stability. Carrying significant debt into retirement can strain your budget and limit your financial flexibility. Prioritize debt repayment to alleviate financial stress and improve your long-term financial outlook.

Ensuring Long-Term Financial Security

Inflation and Healthcare Costs: While addressing short-term needs is vital, it's equally important to plan for the long-term impact of inflation and rising healthcare costs. Over time, the purchasing power of money decreases due to inflation.

Healthcare expenses, in particular, tend to rise as you age. Incorporating inflation-adjusted projections into your retirement plan ensures that your savings will retain their value and adequately support your lifestyle in the future.

Retirement Savings and Investments: Building a robust retirement savings and investment portfolio is the cornerstone of long-term financial security. Consistent contributions to retirement accounts, such as 401(k)s and IRAs, coupled with a diversified investment strategy, can help your savings grow over time.

Longevity Considerations: With increasing life expectancies, planning for a longer retirement period has become essential. Longevity considerations are particularly important if you have a family history of longevity or if you anticipate a healthier lifestyle during retirement.

Preparing for a potentially extended retirement horizon will ensure that you have sufficient resources to maintain your desired lifestyle throughout your golden years.

Social Security and Pension Benefits: Social Security and pension benefits play a crucial role in ensuring long-term financial security for retirees. Delaying Social Security benefits can result in higher monthly payments, providing an additional source of income during retirement. Assess your eligibility for pension benefits and consider how these sources of income fit into your overall retirement plan.

Strategies for Balancing Short-Term Needs with Long-Term Security

Prioritize Budgeting and Saving: Implementing a comprehensive budgeting plan allows you to allocate funds for both short-term expenses and long-term savings. Emphasize the importance of saving for retirement alongside meeting immediate financial needs to maintain a healthy balance.

Automate Retirement Contributions: Set up automatic contributions to your retirement accounts to ensure consistent savings. By automating contributions, you avoid the temptation to spend the funds elsewhere and build a robust retirement nest egg over time.

Review and Adjust Financial Plan: Regularly review your financial plan to ensure that it aligns with your changing circumstances and goals. Life events, such as marriage, the birth of a child, or changes in employment, can impact your financial needs and require adjustments to your plan.

Seek Professional Advice: Consulting with a financial advisor can provide invaluable insights and guidance as you navigate the complexities of balancing short-term needs with long-term security. A financial professional can help you develop a personalized retirement plan that addresses your unique situation and goals.

Balancing short-term needs with long-term security is a critical aspect of creating a comprehensive retirement plan. By addressing immediate financial requirements while safeguarding your future financial well-being, you can build a retirement that is financially resilient and emotionally fulfilling.

Careful planning, budgeting, and prudent decision-making will empower you to embark on a retirement journey that celebrates both the present joys and the promise of a secure and prosperous future.

Developing a Strategic Savings and Investment Strategy

Designing a Diversified Investment Portfolio:

Creating a diversified investment portfolio is an essential pillar of your comprehensive retirement plan. As you embark on your journey of fearless retirement planning, understanding the significance of diversification and its role in optimizing returns while managing risk is vital.

Let's delve deeper into the intricacies of designing a diversified investment portfolio, empowering you to make informed investment decisions that align with your financial goals and risk tolerance.

The Importance of Diversification

Diversification is the practice of spreading your investments across a wide range of asset classes, industries, and geographic regions. The primary objective of diversification is to reduce the impact of individual investment risks on your overall portfolio performance. By diversifying, you aim to achieve a balance between risk and return, ensuring that your portfolio is resilient to market fluctuations and economic uncertainties.

Understanding Asset Classes

Equities (Stocks): Equities represent ownership in a company and are considered a growth-oriented asset class. Stocks have the potential for higher returns over the long term but also carry higher volatility. Within equities, you can invest in individual stocks or opt for exchange-traded funds (ETFs) and mutual funds that provide exposure to a basket of stocks.

Fixed-Income Securities (Bonds): Fixed-income securities are debt instruments issued by governments, municipalities, or corporations. Bonds are generally considered lower risk compared to stocks and provide a steady stream of income through interest payments. Government bonds, corporate bonds, and municipal bonds are common types of fixed-income securities.

Cash and Cash Equivalents: Cash and cash equivalents, such as money market funds, provide liquidity and stability to your portfolio. These assets typically have lower returns than stocks and bonds but offer protection against short-term market fluctuations.

Real Assets: Real assets include physical assets like real estate, commodities, and precious metals. Investing in real assets can provide diversification benefits, as their performance may not always correlate with traditional financial assets like stocks and bonds.

Benefits of Diversification

Risk Reduction: Diversification helps reduce the impact of individual asset performance on your overall portfolio. While some assets may experience losses, others may perform well, balancing out the overall impact on your investments.

Potential for Higher Returns: By allocating funds to different asset classes, you increase the likelihood of capturing the positive performance of various markets. This can lead to potentially higher overall returns compared to investing in just one asset class.

Smoothing Out Market Volatility: Diversification can help smooth out the peaks and valleys of market volatility. When one asset class experiences a decline, other assets in the portfolio may act as a buffer, mitigating the impact on your overall investment performance.

Strategies for Building a Diversified Portfolio:

Asset Allocation: Determine the appropriate allocation of your investment funds across different asset classes based on your financial goals, risk tolerance, and investment time horizon. Younger individuals with a longer investment horizon may opt for a higher allocation to equities, while those closer to retirement may prefer a more conservative allocation.

Geographic Diversification: Invest in companies and assets across various geographic regions to reduce the impact of regional economic fluctuations. International and emerging markets can offer diversification benefits beyond domestic investments.

Sector Allocation: Within equities, consider diversifying across different sectors of the economy, such as technology, healthcare, finance, and energy. This allows you to benefit from the growth potential of various industries while reducing sector-specific risks.

Rebalancing: Regularly review and rebalance your investment portfolio to maintain the desired asset allocation. As certain assets outperform or underperform others, your portfolio's allocation may drift from your original plan. Rebalancing involves selling assets that have appreciated significantly and reinvesting the proceeds into underperforming assets to restore the desired allocation.

Designing a diversified investment portfolio is a fundamental aspect of your comprehensive retirement plan. By spreading your investments across various asset classes, industries, and geographic regions, you can optimize returns while managing risk.

Diversification provides stability during market volatility and ensures that your retirement savings are well-positioned to weather-changing economic conditions.

Maximizing Retirement Account Contributions and Tax Benefits

As you progress on your fearless retirement planning journey, maximizing contributions to your retirement accounts and leveraging tax benefits become powerful tools for building a secure financial future. Retirement accounts offer valuable tax advantages that can significantly enhance your savings and accelerate your path to a comfortable retirement. In this section, we'll explore the strategies and benefits of maximizing retirement account contributions to unlock the full potential of your retirement savings.

Understanding Retirement Accounts:

Traditional 401(k): A traditional 401(k) is an employer-sponsored retirement account that allows you to contribute pre-tax dollars from your paycheck. Contributions to a traditional 401(k) reduce your taxable income for the current year, meaning you pay less in income taxes. However, you'll owe taxes on withdrawals during retirement.

Roth 401(k): Similar to a traditional 401(k), a Roth 401(k) is offered by employers and allows you to contribute after-tax dollars. The advantage of a Roth 401(k) is that qualified withdrawals during retirement are tax-free, providing tax-free income in your golden years.

Traditional IRA: A traditional IRA is an individual retirement account that allows you to make tax-deductible contributions, reducing your taxable income for the current year. Like a traditional 401(k), withdrawals from a traditional IRA during retirement are taxed at your regular income tax rate.

Roth IRA: A Roth IRA is an individual retirement account that permits you to contribute after-tax dollars. Qualified withdrawals from a Roth IRA during retirement are tax-free, offering tax-free income when you need it most.

The Benefits of Maximizing Contributions

Tax Advantages: Maximizing contributions to retirement accounts offers immediate tax benefits. With traditional accounts, your contributions reduce your taxable income, lowering your tax bill for the current year. In Roth accounts, while contributions are made with after-tax dollars, the withdrawals during retirement are tax-free, effectively shielding your savings from future tax liabilities.

Tax-Deferred Growth: Retirement accounts provide tax-deferred growth, meaning that your investments can grow without being subject to annual taxes. Over time, this tax-deferred growth can significantly boost your retirement savings.

Compound Interest: By maximizing contributions early and allowing your investments to benefit from compound interest, your retirement savings have the potential to grow substantially over the years. Compound interest allows your earnings to generate additional earnings, creating a snowball effect that accelerates your wealth accumulation.

Employer Matching: If your employer offers a 401(k) match, maximizing your contributions to the extent of the match is crucial. Employer matching is essentially free money, providing an immediate return on your contributions.

Strategies for Maximizing Contributions

Contribute Regularly and Automatically: Consistency is key to maximizing contributions. Set up automatic contributions to your retirement accounts to ensure that you contribute regularly without the need for manual intervention. Consistent contributions, even in small amounts, can lead to significant savings over time.

Contribute Windfalls: Whenever you receive unexpected windfalls, such as tax refunds or bonuses, consider allocating a portion of these funds to your retirement accounts. Windfalls provide an excellent opportunity to boost your savings without impacting your regular budget.

Catch-Up Contributions: For individuals aged 50 and older, catch-up contributions allow you to contribute additional funds to your retirement accounts above the standard contribution limits. Catch-up contributions provide an opportunity to accelerate your retirement savings in the years leading up to retirement.

Employer Retirement Benefits: Familiarize yourself with all retirement benefits offered by your employer, such as profit-sharing plans or employee stock purchase plans. Taking advantage of these additional benefits can further enhance your retirement savings.

Maximizing retirement account contributions and leveraging tax benefits are integral components of your comprehensive retirement plan. The immediate tax advantages, tax-deferred growth, and compound interest offered by retirement accounts provide the potential for significant wealth accumulation over time. By consistently contributing and taking advantage of employer matching and catch-up contributions, you can build a substantial nest egg to support your desired lifestyle during retirement.

Chapter 3

Navigating Social Security and Medicare

In Chapter 3 of your fearless retirement planning journey, we'll dive into the intricacies of Social Security and Medicare. These vital government programs play a significant role in providing financial support and healthcare coverage during your retirement years. Understanding the nuances of Social Security benefits and making informed decisions about Medicare options will empower you to maximize your financial security and well-being in your golden years.

Understanding Social Security Benefits and Claiming Strategies

Timing Your Social Security Claim for Maximum Payout

Making decisions about when to claim Social Security benefits is a pivotal aspect of your retirement planning. The timing of your claim can significantly impact the amount of money you receive from Social Security each month throughout your retirement. Understanding the nuances of when and how to claim your benefits is essential to maximize your Social Security payout and create a solid financial foundation for your golden years.

The Basics of Social Security Claiming

You become eligible to start claiming Social Security benefits at age 62, but you also have the option to delay your claim up to age 70. Your full retirement age (FRA) depends on your birth year and ranges from 66 to 67. Claiming before your FRA results in a reduction in your monthly benefit, while delaying your claim beyond your FRA leads to an increase in your monthly benefit.

Early vs. Delayed Retirement

Claiming Early (Age 62): Many individuals choose to claim Social Security benefits as soon as they become eligible at age 62. While this option provides immediate income, it comes with a drawback – a permanent reduction in your monthly benefit. If you claim at age 62 and your FRA is 67, your benefit will be approximately 30% lower than what it would be if you had waited until your FRA.

Full Retirement Age (FRA) Claim: Claiming at your FRA ensures that you receive your full benefit amount without any reduction. This option is suitable for those who need the income but don't want to accept the permanent reduction associated with claiming early. However, if you can afford to wait, delaying your claim may yield even more substantial benefits.

Delayed Retirement (Age 70): For every year you delay claiming Social Security between your FRA and age 70, your benefit increases by a certain percentage, known as delayed retirement credits. The increase varies based on your birth year, but it generally ranges from 7% to 8% per year. Delaying your claim until age 70 can result in a significant boost to your monthly benefit, up to 24% to 32% more than your FRA benefit.

Factors to Consider

Financial Situation: Assess your financial needs and overall retirement plan. If you need immediate income to cover expenses, early claiming may be necessary. However, if you have sufficient retirement savings or other sources of income to support you until later in your retirement, delaying your claim can be advantageous.

Health and Longevity: Consider your health and family history of longevity. If you expect to live a long and healthy life, delaying your claim may provide greater cumulative benefits over your lifetime.

Coordinating Spousal and Survivor Benefits

Coordinating Spousal and Survivor Benefits

Coordinating spousal and survivor benefits is a crucial aspect of Social Security planning, particularly for married individuals. Understanding how these benefits work in tandem can help maximize the financial security of both spouses during retirement and provide a safety net in the event of one spouse's passing. In this section, we'll delve into the intricacies of coordinating spousal and survivor benefits, empowering you to optimize your Social Security strategy as a couple.

Spousal Benefits

Spousal benefits allow one spouse to receive a portion of the other spouse's Social Security benefit based on their earnings record. To be eligible for spousal benefits, the lower-earning spouse must be at least 62 years old, and the higher-earning spouse must have already claimed their own Social Security benefits.

Eligibility: Spousal benefits are available to individuals who are currently married, as well as those who are divorced but were married for at least ten years and have not remarried. If both spouses are eligible for their own Social Security benefits, they may choose either their benefit or a spousal benefit, whichever is higher.

Benefit Amount: The spousal benefit amount is typically equal to 50% of the higher-earning spouse's full retirement age (FRA) benefit. For example, if the higher-earning spouse's FRA benefit is $2,000 per month, the lower-earning spouse could receive up to $1,000 per month in spousal benefits. However, to receive the full 50% spousal benefit, the lower-earning spouse must wait until their own FRA to claim it.

Claiming Strategy: For some couples, it may be advantageous for the higher-earning spouse to delay claiming Social Security benefits until age 70 to accrue delayed retirement credits, increasing their benefit. By doing so, they also enhance the potential spousal benefit amount that the lower-earning spouse could receive if they claim spousal benefits at their FRA.

Survivor Benefits

Survivor benefits provide financial support to widows and widowers after the passing of their spouse. These benefits are a critical safety net and can help ensure the surviving spouse's financial well-being during a challenging time.

Eligibility: To be eligible for survivor benefits, the surviving spouse must have been married to the deceased spouse for at least nine months before their passing. However, this requirement is waived if the death was accidental or occurred while serving in the military. If the surviving spouse is caring for a child who is under 16 or disabled, they can be eligible for survivor benefits regardless of how long they were married.

Benefit Amount: The survivor benefit amount is based on the deceased spouse's earnings record. The surviving spouse can receive 100% of the deceased spouse's FRA benefit if they claim survivor benefits at their FRA. If the surviving spouse claims survivor benefits before their FRA, the benefit amount is reduced.

Claiming Strategy: For married couples, the decision about when each spouse claims their own Social Security benefits can significantly impact the survivor benefit. If the higher-earning spouse delays claiming until age 70, it maximizes the potential survivor benefit for the surviving spouse. Coordinating the timing of Social Security claims can ensure that the surviving spouse receives the highest possible benefit amount.

Coordinating Spousal and Survivor Benefits

Coordinating spousal and survivor benefits requires thoughtful planning. For couples with a significant difference in their earnings records, it may be beneficial for the lower-earning spouse to claim spousal benefits while the higher-earning spouse delays claiming their benefits.

This approach allows the lower-earning spouse to receive some income while allowing the higher-earning spouse's benefit to grow through delayed retirement credits.

Additionally, if the higher-earning spouse has a longer life expectancy, they may consider delaying their benefit to increase the potential survivor benefit for their spouse. This strategy can provide greater financial security for the surviving spouse after their partner passes away.

Seek Professional Guidance

Navigating the complexities of coordinating spousal and survivor benefits requires a thorough understanding of Social Security rules and regulations. It's crucial to consult with a financial advisor or Social Security expert to develop a personalized strategy that aligns with your unique circumstances and goals.

By optimizing your Social Security claiming decisions, you can enhance the financial well-being of both spouses and create a secure foundation for your joint retirement journey.

Coordinating spousal and survivor benefits is a valuable component of your comprehensive Social Security planning. By strategically timing your claims and considering each spouse's benefit, you can maximize the potential benefits available to both of you during retirement.

Decoding Medicare Options and Healthcare Coverage

Evaluating Medicare Parts A, B, C, and D

As you approach the age of 65, navigating the world of Medicare becomes essential for comprehensive healthcare coverage during your retirement years. Medicare is a federal health insurance program that offers various parts, each serving different aspects of your healthcare needs. Understanding the components of Medicare—Parts A, B, C, and D—empowers you to make informed decisions about your healthcare coverage and access the medical services you need.

Medicare Part A

Medicare Part A is often referred to as "hospital insurance" and provides coverage for inpatient hospital care, skilled nursing facility care, hospice care, and some home healthcare services. Most individuals do not pay a premium for Part A if they or their spouse paid Medicare taxes while working for a sufficient duration. However, there may be deductibles and coinsurance associated with certain services.

Coverage:

a. Inpatient Hospital Care: Part A covers hospital stays, including semi-private rooms, meals, nursing services, and other medically necessary services during your hospital stay.

b. Skilled Nursing Facility Care: If you require skilled nursing care following a hospital stay, Part A provides coverage for up to 100 days in a skilled nursing facility. To qualify, you must have a qualifying hospital stay and need skilled nursing or rehabilitative services.

c. Hospice Care: Part A covers hospice care for individuals with terminal illnesses, providing comfort and support during the final stages of life.

Medicare Part B

Medicare Part B is known as "medical insurance" and covers a wide range of outpatient services, including doctor visits, preventive services, durable medical equipment, and other medically necessary services. Part B requires a monthly premium, which is typically deducted from your Social Security benefits.

Coverage:

a. Doctor Visits: Part B covers visits to doctors and other healthcare providers, including specialists. It also covers telehealth services, allowing you to receive care remotely in certain situations.

b. Preventive Services: Part B provides coverage for preventive services, such as screenings, vaccinations, and counseling, to help you maintain good health and detect potential health issues early.

c. Durable Medical Equipment (DME): Part B covers medically necessary durable medical equipment, such as wheelchairs, walkers, and oxygen equipment.

Medicare Part C (Medicare Advantage)

Medicare Part C, also known as Medicare Advantage, offers an alternative way to receive Medicare benefits through private insurance plans approved by Medicare. These plans must cover all the services provided by Parts A and B and may include additional benefits like prescription drug coverage, dental, vision, and hearing coverage.

Coverage:

a. All-in-One Coverage: Medicare Advantage plans provide the same coverage as Parts A and B but often offer additional benefits, such as prescription drug coverage, that Original Medicare (Parts A and B) does not include.

b. Network of Providers: Medicare Advantage plans typically have a network of healthcare providers, and you may need to use in-network providers to receive the full benefits of the plan.

c. Costs and Premiums: Medicare Advantage plans may have different costs and premiums, which can vary based on the specific plan and the insurance company offering it.

Medicare Part D

Medicare Part D is prescription drug coverage, available as a standalone plan or as part of a Medicare Advantage plan. Part D helps reduce the cost of prescription medications, ensuring that you have access to the medications you need to manage your health.

Coverage:

a. Prescription Drugs: Part D plans cover a wide range of prescription drugs, including both brand-name and generic medications. The list of covered drugs, known as the formulary, may vary from one plan to another.

b. Tiered Formulary: Part D plans often use a tiered formulary, where medications are grouped into different tiers with different cost-sharing amounts. Generally, generic drugs have lower copayments than brand-name drugs.

c. Coverage Gap (Donut Hole): Part D includes a coverage gap, also known as the "donut hole," where you may pay a higher percentage of the medication costs. Once you reach a certain spending limit, you enter catastrophic coverage, where your out-of-pocket costs decrease significantly.

Assessing Your Healthcare Needs

When evaluating Medicare Parts A, B, C, and D, consider your healthcare needs, budget, and personal preferences. Original Medicare (Parts A and B) provides broad coverage, while Medicare Advantage (Part C) offers additional benefits and may be more suitable if you prefer an all-in-one plan. Part D is essential if you regularly take prescription medications, as it helps manage the cost of your drugs.

Additional Coverage Options

Apart from Medicare, you may consider supplemental insurance, such as Medigap policies, to fill gaps in Original Medicare coverage. Medigap plans help cover out-of-pocket costs like copayments, coinsurance, and deductibles. Additionally, long-term care insurance can provide financial protection for services that Medicare typically does not cover, such as assisted living facilities or nursing home care.

Enrollment and Enrollment Periods

Enrolling in Medicare generally occurs around your 65th birthday, but specific enrollment periods and requirements may vary depending on your circumstances. It's crucial to understand the initial enrollment period, special enrollment periods, and the annual open enrollment period for making changes to your coverage.

Evaluating Medicare Parts A, B, C, and D is a critical step in securing comprehensive healthcare coverage during your retirement. Understanding the coverage options and assessing your healthcare needs will help you make informed decisions about the best Medicare plan(s) for your unique situation.

By navigating the complexities of Medicare, you can access the medical services you need with peace of mind, ensuring a healthy and fulfilling retirement.

Supplemental Medigap and Long-Term Care Insurance Considerations

As you delve into the intricacies of Medicare, it's essential to recognize that while Medicare provides vital healthcare coverage, it may not cover all medical expenses. Supplemental insurance options, such as Medigap policies and long-term care insurance, offer additional layers of protection, filling the gaps left by Medicare. In this section, we'll explore the significance of considering supplemental Medigap and long-term care insurance to ensure comprehensive coverage and financial security in your retirement years.

Medigap Policies

Medigap, also known as Medicare Supplement Insurance, is private insurance designed to help pay for out-of-pocket costs associated with Original Medicare (Parts A and B). Medigap policies are standardized and labeled with letters from A to N, each providing specific coverage options.

Coverage Options:

a. Hospitalization Costs: Medigap policies can cover the coinsurance, copayments, and deductibles for hospital stays under Part A.

b. Medical Costs: Medigap plans can help cover coinsurance and copayments for medical services received under Part B, such as doctor visits and outpatient care.

c. Blood Transfusions: Some Medigap plans to cover the cost of the first three pints of blood, which Original Medicare does not cover.

d. Skilled Nursing Facility Care: Medigap can provide coverage for the coinsurance costs for skilled nursing facility care under Part A.

e. Foreign Travel Emergency: Some Medigap plans offer coverage for emergency medical care during foreign travel.

Choosing the Right Medigap Plan

When evaluating Medigap policies, it's crucial to consider your healthcare needs, budget, and preferred level of coverage. Each standardized plan offers different benefits, and the premiums may vary among insurance providers. Assess your medical history, expected healthcare expenses, and any anticipated travel plans to choose a Medigap plan that aligns with your unique situation.

Long-Term Care Insurance

Long-term care insurance is designed to provide coverage for services not typically covered by Medicare or other health insurance plans. These services include assistance with activities of daily living (ADLs), such as bathing, dressing, eating, and mobility. Long-term care insurance is essential for preserving your savings and assets in the face of potential long-term care expenses.

Coverage Options:

a. In-Home Care: Long-term care insurance may cover in-home care services provided by trained caregivers or home health aides.

b. Assisted Living Facilities: Coverage can extend to assisted living facilities, which offer a higher level of care than living at home but are less intensive than nursing homes.

c. Nursing Home Care: Long-term care insurance can cover the costs of nursing home care, which provides 24/7 medical supervision and skilled nursing care.

d. Adult Day Care: Some policies include coverage for adult day care services, which offer social activities and care during daytime hours.

The Importance of Long-Term Care Planning

The need for long-term care can arise from various factors, such as age, chronic illness, or disabilities. Without adequate insurance coverage, long-term care expenses can quickly deplete your retirement savings and impact your financial security. Long-term care insurance offers peace of mind, knowing that you have financial protection in place for potential future needs.

Enrollment Considerations

Enrolling in Medigap policies and long-term care insurance should be carefully timed. For Medigap, the best time to enroll is during your Medigap open enrollment period, which begins when you turn 65 and are enrolled in Medicare Part B. During this period, you have guaranteed issue rights, meaning that insurance companies cannot deny you coverage or charge you higher premiums based on your health.

For long-term care insurance, consider enrolling at a relatively younger age when premiums are typically lower and you are more likely to meet the health requirements for coverage. Waiting until you are older may result in higher premiums or potential health issues that could disqualify you from coverage.

Seek Professional Guidance

Understanding the intricacies of Medigap and long-term care insurance requires expert guidance. Consult with a licensed insurance agent or financial advisor who specializes in Medicare and long-term care planning to explore your options and choose policies that suit your needs and budget.

Supplemental insurance options, such as Medigap policies and long-term care insurance, play a vital role in ensuring comprehensive healthcare coverage and financial security during your retirement years.

These insurance solutions offer protection against unexpected medical expenses and long-term care costs, preserving your retirement savings for other essential aspects of your life.

Chapter 4

Optimal Tax Planning in Retirement

As you embark on your retirement journey, understanding the intricacies of tax planning is crucial for preserving and maximizing your hard-earned savings. Optimal tax planning can help you minimize tax liabilities, optimize your retirement income, and leave a lasting legacy for your loved ones. In this chapter, we'll explore essential strategies for tax efficiency in retirement, including tax-efficient withdrawal strategies, Roth conversions, estate planning, and legacy preservation.

Utilizing Tax-Efficient Withdrawal Strategies

As you step into your well-deserved retirement, one of the critical challenges is efficiently managing your retirement income and navigating the complex landscape of taxes. To make the most of your hard-earned savings, it's essential to craft a tax-efficient withdrawal strategy. This strategy involves careful consideration of the sequence and timing of withdrawing funds from various retirement accounts, ensuring that you meet your financial needs while minimizing your tax liabilities. Let's delve into the key components of tax-efficient withdrawal strategies and explore how they can optimize your retirement income.

Sequence of Withdrawals

The sequence in which you withdraw funds from your retirement accounts can significantly impact your overall tax situation. The primary goal is to postpone taxes on tax-deferred accounts and leverage tax-free accounts to their fullest potential.

Taxable Accounts: Start by withdrawing funds from taxable accounts, such as regular brokerage accounts or savings accounts. These withdrawals generally do not trigger any tax consequences, as they are already subject to taxes before being invested.

Tax-Deferred Accounts: Move on to tax-deferred accounts, such as traditional IRAs and 401(k)s. Remember that withdrawals from these accounts are taxed as ordinary income. By postponing withdrawals until later in retirement, you may benefit from lower tax rates or avoid pushing your income into higher tax brackets.

Tax-Free Accounts: Finally, if you have a Roth IRA or Roth 401(k), consider leaving these accounts for last. Qualified distributions from Roth accounts are entirely tax-free, providing an excellent source of tax-free income during retirement.

Managing Tax Brackets

Staying within lower tax brackets is a crucial aspect of tax-efficient withdrawal strategies. By carefully managing your withdrawals each year, you can minimize the overall taxes paid on your retirement income.

Partial Withdrawals: Consider withdrawing only the amount you need to cover your living expenses and keeping your taxable income within a lower tax bracket. This approach allows you to preserve a tax-efficient structure for future years.

Mixing Withdrawals: Combining withdrawals from both taxable and tax-deferred accounts can provide flexibility in managing your taxable income. By maintaining a strategic balance, you can optimize your tax situation each year.

Tax-Efficient Investments

Selecting tax-efficient investments is another valuable component of tax planning. Investments like municipal bonds can help reduce the taxable income generated from your investment portfolio.

Municipal Bonds: Interest income from municipal bonds is generally exempt from federal taxes and may be exempt from state taxes if the bonds are issued within your state of residence. These bonds can provide a tax-free income stream, particularly for retirees in higher tax brackets.

Tax-Loss Harvesting: Tax-loss harvesting involves strategically selling investments that have experienced losses to offset capital gains and potentially reduce your taxable income.

Coordinating with Other Income Sources

In addition to your retirement accounts, you may have other sources of income during retirement, such as Social Security benefits or pension payments. Coordinating your withdrawals with these income sources is essential for maintaining a tax-efficient approach.

Social Security Timing: The timing of your Social Security claim can impact your overall tax situation. If possible, consider delaying your Social Security benefits until you reach full retirement age or even beyond, as this can increase your benefit amount and provide a more stable source of income during later years when other accounts may be depleted.

Pension Payout Options: If you have a pension plan, explore the different payout options. Some plans offer the choice between lump sum or annuity payments. Analyze the tax implications of each option and select the one that aligns with your tax planning goals.

Reevaluating Strategies Periodically

Tax laws and your financial situation may change over time, necessitating periodic reevaluation of your tax-efficient withdrawal strategies. It's essential to stay informed about changes in tax regulations and collaborate with your financial advisor to adjust your strategy as needed.

Tax-efficient withdrawal strategies are a critical element of successful retirement planning. By thoughtfully managing the sequence and timing of your withdrawals, considering tax-efficient investments, and coordinating with other income sources, you can minimize your tax burden and make the most of your retirement savings.

Crafting a tax-efficient plan tailored to your unique circumstances can help you achieve your financial goals while enjoying a fulfilling and worry-free retirement.

Minimizing Taxes on Retirement Income and Distributions:

As you embark on the exciting phase of retirement, managing your retirement income effectively while optimizing your tax situation becomes paramount. Minimizing taxes on your retirement income and distributions is a crucial aspect of smart financial planning, ensuring that you retain more of your hard-earned money for the things that matter most in your post-career life. In this chapter, we'll explore practical strategies and real-life examples to help you navigate the complexities of taxation and create a tax-efficient plan for a financially secure retirement.

Social Security Benefits

Social Security benefits form a significant portion of retirement income for many individuals. Understanding how these benefits are taxed and planning your withdrawals accordingly can make a substantial difference in your overall tax liability.

Example:

Let's consider Mary, who has recently retired at age 65 and plans to start receiving Social Security benefits. She has other sources of income, including a pension and investment accounts. Mary's Social Security benefits will be subject to taxation if her provisional income (adjusted gross income + nontaxable interest + half of Social Security benefits) exceeds a certain threshold. To minimize her tax burden, Mary decides to delay claiming Social Security benefits until age 67, allowing her other income sources to bridge the gap.

By doing so, she can stay within a lower tax bracket during the early years of retirement and enjoy more tax-efficient withdrawals.

Pension and Retirement Plan Distributions

Withdrawals from traditional pension plans and tax-deferred retirement accounts, such as traditional IRAs and 401(k)s, are typically taxed as ordinary income. Careful planning of these distributions can help manage your taxable income effectively.

Example:

John, age 68, is retired and relies on his pension and traditional IRA for retirement income. He needs to withdraw funds to cover his living expenses, but he doesn't want to push himself into a higher tax bracket. John decides to withdraw only the required minimum distributions (RMDs) from his traditional IRA each year, keeping his taxable income in the current tax bracket. To supplement his income, John withdraws additional funds from his Roth IRA, which doesn't affect his taxable income. By implementing this strategy, John can optimize his tax situation and retain more of his retirement savings.

Capital Gains and Dividends

Investment income, such as capital gains and dividends, can add to your taxable income. Strategically managing your investment portfolio and taking advantage of tax-efficient investments can help reduce your tax burden.

Example:

Sarah, a retiree, has a diversified investment portfolio consisting of taxable and tax-advantaged accounts. She plans to generate income from her investments while minimizing taxes. To achieve this, Sarah invests in tax-free municipal bonds for her taxable account. The interest income from municipal bonds is typically exempt from federal taxes and may also be exempt from state taxes if issued within her state of residence. Additionally, Sarah focuses on long-term investments to qualify for lower capital gains tax rates. By combining these strategies, Sarah can enjoy tax-efficient investment income during her retirement years.

Roth Conversions and Tax Planning

Roth conversions can be a powerful tool for managing your tax situation in retirement. Converting funds from a traditional IRA to a Roth IRA involves paying taxes on the converted amount upfront but can provide tax-free withdrawals in the future.

Example:

Michael, age 60, has a substantial balance in his traditional IRA but expects to have sufficient income from other sources during the next few years, keeping him in a lower tax bracket. He decides to execute a series of Roth conversions over several years, converting a portion of his traditional IRA to a Roth IRA. By doing so, Michael pays taxes on the converted amount at a lower rate and creates a tax-free income stream for the future. This strategic planning allows him to manage his tax liability efficiently throughout his retirement.

Tax-Loss Harvesting

Tax-loss harvesting involves strategically selling investments that have experienced losses to offset capital gains and potentially reduce your taxable income.

Example:

Anna, a retiree, reviews her investment portfolio and finds that some of her investments have experienced losses due to market fluctuations. She decides to execute tax-loss harvesting by selling those investments to realize the losses. Anna uses these losses to offset capital gains from other investments, reducing her taxable income and potential tax liability. By employing this strategy, Anna can optimize her tax situation and maximize her after-tax returns on her investments.

Minimizing taxes on retirement income and distributions is an integral part of a comprehensive retirement plan. By understanding the tax implications of various income sources, strategically managing withdrawals, leveraging tax-efficient investments, and implementing tax planning strategies like Roth conversions and tax-loss harvesting, you can create a tax-efficient retirement income plan that preserves more of your wealth and enhances your financial security.

As you embark on this chapter of your life, collaborating with a qualified financial advisor can provide valuable guidance and ensure your plan aligns with your unique goals and circumstances.

Roth Conversions and Their Impact on Taxes

As you plan for a financially secure retirement, understanding the role of Roth conversions in your tax strategy is essential. A Roth conversion involves transferring funds from a traditional retirement account, such as a traditional IRA or 401(k), to a Roth account. While this conversion requires paying taxes on the converted amount in the year of the transfer, it can have significant long-term benefits, particularly in terms of tax-free withdrawals during retirement. Let's explore the intricacies of Roth conversions and their impact on your overall tax situation.

Tax Treatment of Roth Conversions

When you initiate a Roth conversion, the amount transferred from your traditional retirement account to a Roth account is considered taxable income for the year of the conversion. This means that the converted amount will be added to your total income, potentially pushing you into a higher tax bracket. It's crucial to factor in this tax liability when deciding on the amount to convert and timing the conversion.

The Decision-making Process

The decision to pursue Roth conversions depends on various factors, including your current and projected tax bracket, financial goals, and the availability of funds to pay the taxes on the conversion. It's essential to assess whether a Roth conversion aligns with your long-term financial objectives and complements your overall retirement income strategy.

Advantages of Roth Conversions

Roth conversions offer several advantages, making them a valuable tool in retirement planning:

Tax-Free Withdrawals: The primary benefit of a Roth conversion is that once the funds are in the Roth account, qualified withdrawals in retirement are entirely tax-free. This can provide significant tax diversification in your retirement income, allowing you to withdraw from both taxable and tax-free sources strategically.

Tax Flexibility: By executing partial Roth conversions over several years, you have the flexibility to manage your tax liability. You can time conversions during years when your income and tax rate are relatively lower, optimizing the tax impact.

No Required Minimum Distributions (RMDs): Unlike traditional retirement accounts, Roth IRAs are not subject to RMDs during the account owner's lifetime. This feature allows you to preserve the funds in your Roth account for as long as you wish, potentially leaving a tax-free legacy for your beneficiaries.

Long-Term Tax Planning: Roth conversions can play a vital role in long-term tax planning, particularly if you anticipate a higher tax rate in the future or expect to have substantial retirement savings. By converting funds early, you lock in a lower tax rate on the conversion amount, potentially avoiding higher tax rates on future distributions.

Impact on Future Retirement Income

When considering Roth conversions, it's essential to evaluate their impact on your future retirement income. Since Roth conversions increase your taxable income in the year of the conversion, they can influence the taxation of other income sources, such as Social Security benefits and investment income.

The 5-Year Rule

Another crucial aspect to understand is the "5-year rule" for Roth conversions. To access tax-free withdrawals of converted funds, you must wait at least five years from the date of the conversion. This rule applies separately to each conversion, meaning you need to track the 5 years for each converted amount.

Recharacterization

In the past, individuals had the option to reverse a Roth conversion through a process called "recharacterization." However, the Tax Cuts and Jobs Act of 2017 eliminated this option for Roth conversions executed after December 31, 2017. As a result, once a Roth conversion is made, it is permanent.

Roth conversions can be a powerful tool in your retirement planning toolkit, offering tax diversification and tax-free withdrawals during retirement. However, they require careful consideration, as they impact your current tax liability and future retirement income.

Assessing your financial situation, tax bracket, and long-term goals is critical before deciding to execute a Roth conversion. As with all aspects of retirement planning, working with a qualified financial advisor can provide valuable insights and help you develop a strategy that aligns with your unique circumstances and aspirations.

By incorporating Roth conversions into your comprehensive retirement plan, you can enhance your tax efficiency, preserve more of your wealth, and create a robust financial foundation for your fearless retirement journey.

Estate Planning and Legacy Preservation:

As you navigate the path of retirement planning, addressing estate planning and legacy preservation is of utmost importance. Estate planning involves making arrangements for the management and distribution of your assets after your passing, ensuring that your hard-earned wealth is transferred to your chosen beneficiaries in a smooth and tax-efficient manner.

In this chapter, we will delve into the significance of estate planning and legacy preservation and explore essential components to secure your financial legacy for generations to come.

Minimizing Estate Taxes and Probate Costs:

One of the key objectives of estate planning is to minimize estate taxes and probate costs, which can erode a substantial portion of your estate. By carefully structuring your estate plan, you can take advantage of various strategies to reduce these expenses.

i. Estate Tax Planning:

Estate taxes are imposed on the transfer of your assets after your passing, depending on the value of your estate and the prevailing tax laws. Implementing tax-efficient strategies, such as gifting, establishing trusts, and leveraging marital deductions, can help minimize estate taxes.

ii. Avoiding Probate:

Probate is the legal process of authenticating a will and distributing the assets of a deceased individual. It can be time-consuming, costly, and subject to public records. Proper estate planning can help avoid probate, ensuring that your assets are transferred directly to your beneficiaries without the need for court involvement.

Establishing Trusts and Gifting Strategies for Beneficiaries:

Trusts are powerful tools that can play a crucial role in estate planning and legacy preservation. By setting up trusts, you can exercise greater control over the distribution of your assets, protect your wealth from creditors, and safeguard your legacy.

i. Revocable Living Trust:

A revocable living trust allows you to retain control of your assets during your lifetime while designating beneficiaries to receive those assets upon your passing. Since the trust is revocable, you can make changes or revoke it if your circumstances change.

ii. Irrevocable Trust:

Unlike a revocable living trust, an irrevocable trust cannot be altered or revoked once established. These trusts are often used for tax planning purposes and to protect assets from estate taxes and creditors.

iii. Charitable Trust:

A charitable trust allows you to leave a portion of your estate to a charitable organization, contributing to a cause that holds significance to you while potentially providing tax benefits.

iv. Lifetime Gifting:

Gifting during your lifetime can be an effective strategy to transfer wealth to your beneficiaries while potentially reducing estate taxes. By gifting assets to your loved ones, you can also witness the impact of your generosity and enjoy the satisfaction of providing financial support.

Writing a Comprehensive Will

A will is a fundamental document in estate planning that outlines your wishes for the distribution of your assets and the appointment of guardians for minor children. A well-crafted will ensures that your intentions are legally binding and can help prevent potential disputes among family members.

i. Executor Designation:

Appointing an executor in your will is crucial as this individual will be responsible for administering your estate, distributing assets, and handling any outstanding debts or legal matters.

ii. Guardianship Provisions:

If you have minor children, your will should include provisions for the appointment of guardians who will be responsible for their care and upbringing in the event of your passing.

iii. Residuary Clause:

The residuary clause in your will ensures that any assets not specifically mentioned in the will are distributed according to your wishes.

Regularly Updating Your Estate Plan

Life is dynamic, and circumstances can change over time. Regularly reviewing and updating your estate plan is essential to ensure it remains aligned with your current goals and family situation.

i. Major Life Events:

Marriage, divorce, the birth of children, or the passing of a loved one can significantly impact your estate plan. It's crucial to update your plan to reflect these changes and adjust beneficiary designations as needed.

ii. Tax Law Changes:

Tax laws are subject to amendments, which can influence the effectiveness of your estate planning strategies. Staying informed about tax law changes and collaborating with your estate planning attorney and financial advisor can help you adapt your plan accordingly.

Estate planning and legacy preservation are essential elements of a comprehensive retirement plan. By strategically minimizing estate taxes and probate costs, establishing trusts and gifting strategies, crafting a comprehensive will, and regularly updating your estate plan, you can secure your financial legacy and ensure that your assets are distributed according to your wishes.

Collaborating with experienced estate planning professionals will provide valuable guidance and ensure that your plan is robust, efficient, and tailored to meet the unique needs of your family. Embracing estate planning as part of your fearless retirement journey allows you to leave a lasting impact on your loved ones and generations to come.

Chapter 5

Managing Debt and Housing in Retirement

Strategies for Eliminating Debt Before Retirement

As you approach retirement, managing debt and making informed decisions about housing become critical components of a successful and worry-free retirement plan. In this chapter, we will explore effective strategies for eliminating debt before retirement, enabling you to enter this new phase of life with financial freedom and peace of mind. Additionally, we will delve into evaluating housing options that best suit the needs of 50+ individuals, ensuring that your home complements your retirement lifestyle and financial goals.

Prioritizing Debt Repayment and Debt Snowball Method:

Debt can be a significant financial burden, especially as you approach retirement. It's essential to tackle outstanding debts strategically to enter retirement with greater financial security. One effective approach to debt repayment is prioritizing your debts and adopting the debt snowball method.

Assessing Your Debts: The first step in prioritizing debt repayment is to assess all your outstanding debts. Make a list of your debts, including credit card balances, personal loans, car loans, and any other obligations. Note down the outstanding balances, interest rates, and minimum monthly payments for each debt.

Creating a Budget: Establishing a comprehensive budget is vital in managing your finances effectively. Determine your monthly income, including retirement income sources and any other earnings. Next, list all your essential expenses, such as housing, utilities, food, and healthcare. Allocate a portion of your budget to debt repayment.

Identifying High-Interest Debts: High-interest debts, such as credit card debts, typically have higher interest rates and can cost you more in the long run. These should be the primary focus of your debt repayment plan. While it's essential to continue making at least minimum payments on all debts, allocate extra funds to pay off high-interest debts faster.

The Debt Snowball Method: The debt snowball method, popularized by financial expert Dave Ramsey, involves prioritizing your debts based on their balances, rather than interest rates. Start by paying off the smallest debt first, while continuing to make minimum payments on all other debts.

Once the smallest debt is paid off, use the funds that were going towards it to pay off the next smallest debt. This process continues until all debts are repaid. The snowball effect comes into play as you gain momentum by eliminating smaller debts, which motivates you to tackle larger ones.

Example:

Let's consider an individual, Sarah, who is approaching retirement with several debts, including a $3,000 credit card balance (at 18% interest), a $10,000 personal loan (at 10% interest), and a $20,000 car loan (at 6% interest). Sarah has a monthly budget surplus of $500 that she can allocate toward debt repayment. Following the debt snowball method, Sarah would prioritize paying off the $3,000 credit card debt first. Once that is paid off, she would move on to the $10,000 personal loan, and finally, the $20,000 car loan. By focusing on one debt at a time, Sarah can gain momentum and achieve a sense of accomplishment with each debt she pays off.

Commitment and Persistence: Eliminating debt requires discipline and commitment. Stick to your budget and debt repayment plan consistently, and avoid accumulating new debts. Celebrate your progress along the way, and remind yourself of the financial freedom that awaits you in retirement as you become debt-free.

Prioritizing debt repayment and adopting the debt snowball method are powerful strategies to eliminate debt before retirement. By creating a budget, identifying high-interest debts, and following the debt snowball approach, you can take control of your finances and enter retirement with reduced financial burdens.

Remember that every step towards debt freedom brings you closer to a retirement filled with greater financial security and freedom.

Refinancing Options and Debt Consolidation Considerations

As you prepare for retirement, exploring refinancing options and debt consolidation strategies can be effective in managing your debt more efficiently and reducing financial stress. These methods offer the opportunity to streamline your debt obligations and potentially secure more favorable terms, making it easier to achieve debt freedom before entering retirement.

Understanding Refinancing: Refinancing involves replacing an existing loan or debt with a new loan that has different terms. The primary goal of refinancing is often to obtain a lower interest rate, which can lead to reduced monthly payments and long-term interest costs.

When to Consider Refinancing: Refinancing is a viable option when market interest rates are lower than the rates on your current loans. It's especially beneficial for high-interest debts, such as credit card balances or personal loans.

By refinancing at a lower rate, more of your monthly payment goes toward reducing the principal amount owed, accelerating your journey toward debt freedom.

Mortgage Refinancing: For homeowners, mortgage refinancing can be an essential tool in debt management. If you have a mortgage with a higher interest rate, refinancing to a lower rate can lead to substantial savings over the life of the loan. Additionally, homeowners with sufficient equity may consider a cash-out refinance, where they borrow against the equity in their home to pay off higher-interest debts.

Pros and Cons of Refinancing: While refinancing offers various benefits, it's essential to weigh the pros and cons before proceeding. Lower interest rates and reduced monthly payments are clear advantages. However, keep in mind that refinancing may involve closing costs and fees.

Evaluate the potential savings against the costs to determine if refinancing is the right choice for your financial situation.

Debt Consolidation: Debt consolidation involves combining multiple debts into a single loan or line of credit. This consolidation simplifies debt management, as you only need to make one monthly payment instead of multiple payments to various creditors.

Consolidation Options: There are several ways to consolidate debts, including personal loans, home equity loans or lines of credit (HELOCs), and balance transfer credit cards. The best option depends on your credit score, available equity, and the interest rates offered.

Example:

Let's consider an individual, John, who is nearing retirement with credit card debts, a personal loan, and an outstanding car loan. John has a good credit score and sufficient home equity. He decides to explore debt consolidation by taking out a home equity line of credit (HELOC) with a lower interest rate than his existing debts. With the HELOC, John pays off his credit card debts and personal loan, leaving him with a single monthly payment on the HELOC, which is more manageable and has a lower interest rate than his previous debts.

Refinancing options and debt consolidation are valuable strategies for managing debt effectively before retirement. By refinancing high-interest debts and exploring consolidation options, you can reduce interest costs, simplify debt management, and create a clear path to becoming debt-free before entering retirement.

However, it's crucial to carefully assess the terms and costs associated with refinancing or consolidation to ensure that it aligns with your financial goals. With the right approach and strategic debt management, you can achieve a debt-free retirement, allowing you to focus on enjoying your newfound financial freedom and pursuing the retirement lifestyle you desire.

Evaluating Housing Options for 50+ Individuals

Downsizing, Relocation, and Age-Appropriate Housing

As you approach retirement, making informed decisions about your housing situation becomes vital to ensure that your home aligns with your changing lifestyle and financial goals. The 50+ age group often contemplates downsizing, relocating, or considering age-appropriate housing options to optimize their living arrangements and enhance their retirement experience.

The Significance of Housing Decisions in Retirement: Housing is not only a place to call home; it represents a significant portion of your assets and expenses. Evaluating your housing options in light of your retirement plans is essential for financial preparedness and emotional well-being.

The Benefits of Downsizing: Many individuals in their 50s and beyond choose to downsize their homes as they transition into retirement. Downsizing involves moving from a larger home to a smaller, more manageable property. The benefits of downsizing are multi-fold:

Reduced Maintenance: Smaller homes generally require less maintenance, freeing up your time and energy to focus on activities you enjoy during retirement.

Lower Expenses: Downsizing often results in reduced utility bills, property taxes, and homeowner's insurance costs, allowing you to redirect those savings toward other retirement priorities.

Unlocking Home Equity: Selling a larger home can provide a significant amount of home equity, which can be used to fund retirement expenses, invest, or pursue other financial goals.

Relocating for Lifestyle and Cost Considerations: Some individuals consider relocating to a different city, state, or even country in retirement. Relocation decisions may be driven by lifestyle preferences, a desire to be closer to family, or seeking a more affordable location with a lower cost of living.

Lifestyle Considerations: Retirement presents an opportunity to live in a location that aligns with your interests and passions. Whether it's living near the ocean, in a vibrant city, or serene countryside, the right location can enhance your retirement experience.

Financial Considerations: Relocating to an area with a lower cost of living can stretch your retirement savings further and reduce day-to-day expenses.

Age-Appropriate Housing Options: Aging gracefully often involves considering housing options that cater to changing physical needs and offer supportive communities.

Single-Level Living: Homes with single-level layouts or those equipped with elevators can provide greater accessibility and convenience, particularly if mobility becomes a concern.

Age-Restricted Communities: Age-restricted communities cater specifically to the needs and preferences of older adults. These communities often offer amenities, social activities, and services tailored to retirees.

Continuing Care Retirement Communities (CCRCs): CCRCs provide various levels of care, ranging from independent living to assisted living and skilled nursing care. This continuum of care allows residents to age in place and receive the necessary support as their needs change.

The Emotional Aspect of Housing Decisions: Moving or making significant housing changes in retirement can evoke a mix of emotions. It's essential to give yourself ample time to consider these decisions and to involve family members or trusted advisors in the process.

Example:

Consider Laura, a 50+ individual who is retiring and currently lives in a large suburban home. Laura's children have moved out, and she finds the maintenance and expenses of her home burdensome. After careful consideration, Laura decides to downsize to a smaller townhome in a vibrant city near her favorite cultural venues. This move not only reduces her housing-related expenses but also allows her to live in a community that suits her interests and offers a more active and social lifestyle.

As you approach retirement, evaluating your housing options becomes essential in aligning your home with your retirement lifestyle and financial objectives. Whether you choose to downsize, relocate, or explore age-appropriate housing, these decisions can have a significant impact on your financial well-being and overall retirement experience.

By carefully considering your priorities and involving trusted advisors, you can make informed housing decisions that pave the way for a fulfilling and worry-free retirement. Remember that your home is a reflection of your retirement dreams, and finding the right fit can contribute to a joyful and purposeful chapter in your life.

Utilizing Home Equity and Reverse Mortgages Wisely

For many individuals in their 50s and beyond, homeownership represents a significant portion of their wealth and assets. Utilizing home equity and considering reverse mortgages thoughtfully can offer financial flexibility and support retirement goals. However, it's essential to approach these options with a clear understanding of the implications and potential risks.

Understanding Home Equity: Home equity is the difference between the current market value of your home and the outstanding balance on your mortgage. As you make mortgage payments and property values appreciate, your home equity grows.

Accessing Home Equity: There are several ways to access your home equity:

Home Equity Loan: A home equity loan, also known as a second mortgage, allows you to borrow a lump sum against your home equity. The loan is repaid in fixed installments over a predetermined term.

Home Equity Line of Credit (HELOC): A HELOC provides a revolving line of credit against your home equity. You can borrow as needed, similar to a credit card, and repay the borrowed amount over time.

Utilizing Home Equity Wisely: Before tapping into your home equity, consider your financial objectives and the potential impact on your retirement plan.

Debt Consolidation: Using a home equity loan or HELOC to consolidate high-interest debts can be a strategic move to reduce interest costs and simplify debt management. However, exercise caution to avoid accumulating new debts.

Home Renovations and Improvements: Investing in home improvements can enhance your living space and potentially increase the value of your property. Before proceeding, evaluate the expected return on investment and the impact on your overall financial plan.

Supplementing Retirement Income: Some retirees use home equity to supplement their retirement income. However, ensure that the additional income aligns with your long-term financial needs and that you have a repayment plan in place.

Understanding Reverse Mortgages: A reverse mortgage is a financial product available to homeowners aged 62 and older. It allows you to convert a portion of your home equity into loan proceeds without the requirement of making monthly mortgage payments. The loan is typically repaid when you move out of the home or pass away, and the home is sold.

Pros and Cons of Reverse Mortgages: Reverse mortgages can provide financial relief for retirees with limited income, allowing them to remain in their homes while accessing additional funds. However, it's essential to consider the following aspects:

Loan Costs and Fees: Reverse mortgages often come with upfront fees and closing costs. Be aware of the fees involved and understand how they impact the loan amount.

Impact on Heirs: With a reverse mortgage, the loan becomes due when the homeowner passes away or moves out of the home. If you have heirs, they will need to handle the loan repayment or decide whether to sell the home to settle the debt.

Long-Term Implications: While a reverse mortgage can provide immediate financial relief, carefully assess the long-term impact on your overall retirement plan and potential future housing needs.

For example, imagine John, a 65-year-old retiree, who owns a home with substantial equity. John is interested in pursuing his passion for travel during retirement but has limited liquid assets. He considers a reverse mortgage to supplement his retirement income, allowing him to fund his travel adventures without selling his home. John consults with a financial advisor to assess the long-term implications and ensure that this strategy aligns with his broader financial goals.

Utilizing home equity and considering reverse mortgages can offer financial flexibility and support various retirement goals. Whether you choose to access home equity for debt consolidation, home improvements, or supplementing retirement income, thoughtful planning is essential.

When considering a reverse mortgage, carefully weigh the benefits against the potential risks and assess the impact on your long-term financial security and your heirs. By making informed and strategic decisions about your home equity, you can enhance your retirement experience and make the most of your home's value while preserving financial stability for the years to come.

Chapter 6

Generating Passive Income in Retirement

As you transition into retirement, creating passive income streams becomes a valuable strategy to bolster your financial security and maintain a comfortable lifestyle. Passive income refers to money earned with minimal ongoing effort and active involvement. In this chapter, we will explore various passive income opportunities that can help supplement your retirement savings and provide a steady stream of income without significant time commitment.

Exploring Various Passive Income Streams

Rental Properties and Real Estate Investment

Real estate investment has long been considered a lucrative option for generating passive income, and it remains an attractive strategy for retirees seeking to secure their financial future. Rental properties offer a reliable source of income and the potential for long-term appreciation. Let's delve deeper into the world of real estate investment and how it can benefit retirees.

The Appeal of Rental Properties

Steady Rental Income: One of the primary attractions of rental properties is the consistent cash flow generated from rental payments. As a retiree, having a steady income stream can provide financial stability and peace of mind.

Asset Appreciation: Real estate has historically appreciated over time, which means the value of your property could increase. This potential appreciation adds another layer of financial security to your investment.

Tax Advantages: Real estate investment offers several tax benefits, including deductions for mortgage interest, property taxes, and certain property-related expenses. These deductions can help reduce your overall tax burden.

Inflation Hedge: Rental income has the potential to keep pace with inflation, providing you with a reliable income stream that retains its value over time.

Investing in Rental Properties

Location, Location, Location: When considering rental properties, location is crucial. Look for properties in areas with strong rental demand, good infrastructure, and growth potential. Proximity to amenities, schools, public transportation, and employment centers can make a property more appealing to potential tenants.

Cash Flow Analysis: Conduct a thorough cash flow analysis before purchasing a rental property. Consider all expenses, including mortgage payments, property taxes, insurance, maintenance costs, and property management fees if applicable. Ensure that the rental income exceeds these expenses to generate positive cash flow.

Property Management: As a retiree, you may prefer a hands-off approach to property management. Hiring a professional property management company can take care of tenant screening, rent collection, property maintenance, and other day-to-day responsibilities.

Real Estate Investment Trusts (REITs)

Diversification and Ease of Access: For retirees who prefer not to own physical properties, Real Estate Investment Trusts (REITs) offer an alternative. REITs are companies that own and operate income-generating real estate, such as commercial properties, apartments, and shopping centers. Investing in REITs provides exposure to real estate without the need for property management.

Liquidity: REITs are publicly traded on stock exchanges, providing liquidity that owning physical properties may not offer. You can easily buy and sell shares of REITs, which provides flexibility in managing your investment portfolio.

Risk Considerations

Market Fluctuations: Real estate, like any investment, is subject to market fluctuations. Property values may go up or down based on various factors, including the economy, local housing market conditions, and interest rates. Long-term investment horizons can help mitigate the impact of short-term market fluctuations.

Tenant Turnover: Rental properties may experience periods of vacancy between tenants, which could temporarily affect your rental income. Maintaining cash reserves can help cover expenses during these periods.

Legal and Regulatory Matters: Being a landlord comes with legal responsibilities and obligations. Familiarize yourself with local rental laws and regulations to ensure compliance and protect your interests.

Example:

Consider Susan, a retiree who decides to invest in a rental property in a growing urban area with high demand for rental housing. She purchases a condominium that is easily accessible to public transportation, universities, and job centers. Susan hires a property management company to handle tenant selection, rent collection, and property maintenance. With positive cash flow from the rental income, Susan enjoys financial security and the potential for property appreciation over time.

Rental properties and real estate investment offer retirees a proven path to generate passive income and build wealth. Whether you choose to invest in physical rental properties or opt for the convenience of REITs, real estate can play a significant role in diversifying your investment portfolio and providing consistent cash flow during retirement.

To make informed decisions, conduct thorough research, seek advice from financial experts, and consider your risk tolerance and long-term financial goals. A well-planned real estate investment can contribute to a financially rewarding and fulfilling retirement journey.

Dividend Stocks, Bonds, and Peer-to-Peer Lending

Diversifying your passive income portfolio with a mix of dividend stocks, bonds, and peer-to-peer lending can be an effective strategy to secure a stable income stream during retirement. These investment options offer varying risk profiles and potential returns, allowing you to tailor your portfolio to align with your financial goals and risk tolerance.

Dividend Stocks

What Are Dividend Stocks? Dividend stocks are shares of companies that distribute a portion of their profits to shareholders in the form of dividends. These dividends are typically paid regularly, such as quarterly or annually.

Stability and Income Generation: Dividend stocks are often associated with established and financially sound companies. Investing in dividend-paying companies can provide a steady income stream, especially during times of market volatility.

Dividend Yield: The dividend yield is a key metric that indicates the dividend income relative to the stock price. It is calculated by dividing the annual dividend per share by the stock's current price. A higher dividend yield may indicate a more attractive income-generating opportunity.

Dividend Reinvestment Plans (DRIPs): Some companies offer DRIPs, which allow shareholders to reinvest their dividends to purchase additional shares of the company's stock. This can compound the growth of your investment over time.

Bonds

What Are Bonds? Bonds are debt securities issued by governments, municipalities, or corporations to raise capital. When you invest in bonds, you are essentially lending money to the issuer in exchange for regular interest payments and the return of the principal amount at the bond's maturity.

Fixed Income Stream: Bonds are known for providing a predictable and fixed income stream. Interest payments, also known as coupon payments, are generally paid at regular intervals, such as semi-annually or annually.

Risk and Safety: Bonds are generally considered less risky than stocks, especially if you invest in high-quality government or corporate bonds. However, it's essential to understand that bond prices can fluctuate based on interest rate changes and other market conditions.

Bond Laddering: Building a bond ladder involves investing in bonds with staggered maturities. This strategy provides flexibility, as bonds mature at different intervals, allowing you to reinvest in new bonds or access funds when needed.

Peer-to-Peer Lending

What Is Peer-to-Peer Lending? Peer-to-peer (P2P) lending platforms connect individual investors with borrowers in need of personal or business loans. By participating in P2P lending, you act as a lender and earn interest on the loans you fund.

Potential Returns: P2P lending can offer attractive returns compared to traditional fixed-income investments.

However, it's essential to recognize that higher returns come with higher risks, as P2P loans are typically unsecured and subject to borrower credit risk.

Diversification: To mitigate risk, consider diversifying your P2P lending portfolio by spreading your investments across multiple loans and borrowers.

Due Diligence: Before investing in P2P lending, conduct thorough due diligence on the platform's track record, borrower risk assessment, and default rate.

Example:

Consider Michael, a retiree who seeks to build a balanced passive income portfolio. He allocates a portion of his investment funds to dividend stocks of reputable companies known for consistent dividend payments. To ensure stability, Michael also invests in high-quality government bonds, which provide a predictable income stream and act as a hedge against market fluctuations. Additionally, he explores the potential of P2P lending to earn higher returns but does so by diversifying his investments across various loans and carefully assessing borrower creditworthiness.

Diversifying your passive income portfolio with dividend stocks, bonds, and peer-to-peer lending can be a prudent approach to generating consistent income during retirement. Dividend stocks offer stable income and the potential for capital appreciation, while bonds provide fixed income with varying risk profiles.

P2P lending presents an opportunity for potentially higher returns, but it requires careful risk management and due diligence. By combining these investment options strategically, you can build a well-rounded passive income portfolio that complements your financial objectives and ensures a reliable income stream throughout your retirement journey.

As with any investment strategy, it's crucial to consult with a financial advisor to tailor your portfolio to your specific needs and goals.

Entrepreneurial Ventures and Part-Time Work Opportunities

Turning Hobbies and Skills into Profitable Ventures

Retirement opens the door to a new chapter of life, where you have the freedom to explore your passions and interests without the constraints of a traditional career. Many retirees find joy and fulfillment in turning their hobbies and skills into profitable ventures, allowing them to generate passive income while doing what they love. Let's delve into the world of entrepreneurial pursuits and discover how you can transform your hobbies and expertise into profitable sources of income.

Identifying Your Passions and Talents

Soul Searching: Start by reflecting on your hobbies, interests, and skills that bring you joy and fulfillment. Consider activities you are naturally drawn to and have a genuine passion for.

Recognizing Market Demand: While pursuing your passions is essential, it's equally important to assess whether there is a market demand for your product or service. Research the target audience, potential competition, and market trends to identify viable opportunities.

Monetizing Your Hobbies and Skills

Creating Unique Products: If you have a talent for crafts, art, or handmade products, consider creating unique items that resonate with your target audience. Platforms like Etsy, eBay, and local craft markets provide avenues to showcase and sell your creations.

Teaching and Workshops: Share your expertise and knowledge with others through teaching and workshops. Whether you are skilled in cooking, photography, writing, or any other field, there are individuals eager to learn from you.

Online Courses and Tutorials: Embrace the digital age by creating online courses or tutorials. Platforms like Udemy, Teachable, and Skillshare allow you to reach a global audience and monetize your skills through digital education.

Building Your Brand and Online Presence

Crafting Your Brand Identity: Establish a unique brand identity that reflects your values and resonates with your target audience. Your brand should convey a clear message about what makes your products or services special.

Creating a website or Blog: A well-designed website or blog can serve as your online storefront, allowing potential customers to learn more about your offerings and make purchases directly.

Leveraging social media: Social media platforms provide valuable marketing tools to showcase your work, interact with your audience, and build a community around your brand.

Scaling Your Venture

Balancing Supply and Demand: As your venture grows, carefully manage the supply of your products or services to meet increasing demand. Strive for consistency and quality to maintain customer satisfaction.

Outsourcing and Collaboration: Consider outsourcing certain tasks or collaborating with others to expand your business without overwhelming yourself. Partnerships can bring fresh ideas and shared resources to your venture.

Financial Considerations

Start-Up Costs: Evaluate the initial investment required to kickstart your venture. Keep in mind that some businesses may require more significant capital, while others can be launched with minimal costs.

Pricing Your Offerings: Set prices that are competitive yet reflective of the value you provide. Consider factors like production costs, market demand, and the perceived worth of your products or services.

Example:

Imagine Susan, a retired art teacher with a passion for watercolor painting. She decides to turn her love for painting into a profitable venture by creating a line of unique watercolor greeting cards. Susan sets up an online store to sell her cards and shares her artistic journey on social media. Her art gains traction, and soon, she receives requests for watercolor painting workshops from art enthusiasts. Susan seizes the opportunity to offer online art workshops, expanding her venture into digital education.

Transforming your hobbies and skills into profitable ventures can be a rewarding way to generate passive income in retirement. By tapping into your passions and leveraging your expertise, you not only create an additional income stream but also find purpose and fulfillment in your post-retirement life.

As you embark on this entrepreneurial journey, remember to identify market demand, build a strong brand and online presence, and carefully manage the financial aspects of your venture. With dedication, creativity, and a clear vision, you can turn your hobbies into a thriving and financially rewarding venture during your retirement years.

Freelancing and Consulting in Retirement

Retirement offers the freedom to explore new opportunities, and for many retirees, freelancing and consulting provides an avenue to share their expertise while generating passive income. Whether you want to continue working in your field of expertise or explore new areas, freelancing and consulting offer flexibility, autonomy, and the opportunity to create a fulfilling and financially rewarding retirement.

Let's delve into the world of freelancing and consulting and discover how you can leverage your skills and knowledge in this exciting chapter of life.

Identifying Your Expertise and Niche

Drawing on Your Career Experience: Reflect on your career accomplishments and the valuable skills you developed over the years. Consider the areas where you excelled and the expertise you can offer to others.

Identifying Your Niche: Focus on a specific niche or area of specialization that aligns with your passions and where there is demand for your services. A well-defined niche can set you apart from competitors and attract your ideal clients.

Freelancing in Retirement

Flexibility and Autonomy: Freelancing allows you to set your schedule and work on projects that interest you. As a retiree, you can choose the level of commitment that suits your lifestyle and preferences.

Portfolio Career: Embrace a portfolio career by taking on diverse projects across different industries or skill areas. This approach can keep your work engaging and provide exposure to various opportunities.

Online Freelance Platforms: Websites like Upwork, Fiverr, and Freelancer offer a platform to connect with clients and showcase your skills. Create a compelling profile that highlights your expertise and previous work to attract potential clients.

Consulting in Retirement

Leveraging Your Knowledge: Consulting allows you to leverage your in-depth knowledge and experience to help businesses and individuals overcome challenges and achieve their goals.

Networking and Relationships: Building a strong network of contacts and maintaining professional relationships can lead to consulting opportunities through word-of-mouth referrals and recommendations.

Creating Consulting Packages: Offer consulting packages that clearly outline the scope of your services and the value you provide. This approach makes it easier for clients to understand what to expect and simplifies the negotiation process.

Online Presence and Marketing

Building Your Brand: Establish a strong personal brand that showcases your expertise, credibility, and the benefits clients can gain from working with you.

Online Portfolio and Testimonials: Create an online portfolio that showcases your past projects, achievements, and client testimonials. Positive feedback from previous clients can instill confidence in potential clients.

Content Marketing: Share your knowledge and insights through blog posts, articles, or videos. Content marketing establishes you as an authority in your field and attracts clients seeking your expertise.

Setting Fees and Contracts

Determining Your Value: Assess the value you bring to clients based on your expertise and the impact of your services. Set fees that reflect the value you provide while remaining competitive in the market.

Clear Contracts: When working with clients, use clear and detailed contracts that outline the scope of work, deliverables, timelines, and payment terms. A well-defined contract protects both parties and prevents misunderstandings.

Example:

Imagine John, a retired marketing executive with extensive experience in digital marketing. John decides to start a freelance marketing consultancy, offering his expertise to small businesses seeking to enhance their online presence. He creates an online profile on various freelance platforms and begins networking with local businesses. As word spreads about his expertise and the success stories of his clients, John's consultancy gains momentum, and he finds fulfillment in helping businesses achieve their marketing goals.

Freelancing and consulting offer retirees an exciting opportunity to leverage their expertise, pursue their passions, and generate passive income during retirement. Whether you choose to take on freelance projects or provide consulting services, these flexible and autonomous career paths allow you to work on your terms and maintain a fulfilling retirement lifestyle.

Building a strong online presence, networking, and effectively marketing your services are essential steps in attracting clients and ensuring the success of your freelancing or consulting venture. By leveraging your skills and knowledge in this new chapter of life, you can create a meaningful and financially rewarding retirement journey.

Chapter 7

Embracing a Purposeful Retirement Lifestyle

Retirement is an exciting chapter of life where you have the opportunity to explore new passions, embrace meaningful activities, and create a purposeful and fulfilling lifestyle. This chapter delves into how you can make the most of your retirement years by identifying your passions, engaging in meaningful activities, prioritizing physical and mental well-being, and embarking on memorable adventures, including travel and even considering international retirement options.

Identifying Your Passion and Interests in Retirement

Retirement opens the door to pursue activities that truly bring joy and fulfillment. Take the time to identify your passions and interests to shape a purposeful retirement lifestyle.

Reflecting on Personal Passions: Think about activities or hobbies that you always wanted to explore but may not have had the time for during your working years. It could be painting, gardening, photography, cooking, playing a musical instrument, or anything that sparks your curiosity.

Volunteer Opportunities: Volunteering can provide a sense of purpose and give back to the community. Explore local organizations or causes that resonate with you and consider how you can contribute your time and skills.

Lifelong Learning: Enroll in classes or workshops to continue learning and expanding your knowledge. Lifelong learning not only keeps your mind sharp but also opens up new avenues for personal growth.

Pursuing Meaningful Activities and Volunteer Opportunities

Retirement is not only a time for relaxation but also an opportunity to engage in activities that bring a sense of purpose and fulfillment to your life. Pursuing meaningful activities and volunteering can not only benefit others but also contribute to your well-being and sense of fulfillment during retirement.

Community Involvement and Clubs

One way to stay engaged and make a positive impact in your community is by getting involved in local clubs and organizations. Whether it's a book club, gardening group, or community service organization, being part of a community provides a sense of belonging and fosters meaningful connections with like-minded individuals.

Book Clubs: If you have a passion for literature, joining a book club allows you to read and discuss books with others, fostering intellectual stimulation and social interaction.

Gardening Groups: For nature enthusiasts, gardening groups offer opportunities to beautify the community, share gardening tips, and bond over a shared love of plants and outdoor activities.

Community Service Organizations: Volunteering with community service organizations allows you to contribute to causes that matter to you, such as feeding the homeless, mentoring at-risk youth, or supporting local environmental initiatives.

Mentoring and Passing on Knowledge

Your wealth of experience and knowledge gained over the years can be a valuable resource for others. Consider mentoring younger individuals, college students, or professionals starting their careers. Sharing your wisdom and insights not only benefits mentees but also provides a sense of purpose and satisfaction in passing on knowledge.

Mentoring Students: Many schools and universities offer mentoring programs where retirees can provide guidance and support to students pursuing similar career paths.

Professional Mentoring: If you had a successful career in a specific industry, consider offering your expertise as a consultant or advisor to entrepreneurs or startups.

Charitable Activities and Helping Others

Retirement is an excellent time to give back to the community and support charitable causes that align with your values and interests.

Volunteering at Local Charities: Explore volunteer opportunities with local charities, shelters, or food banks. Helping those in need can provide a profound sense of fulfillment and purpose.

Supporting Causes You're Passionate About Whether it's animal welfare, education, or healthcare, consider contributing to causes that resonate with you. Donating time or funds can make a significant impact and bring a sense of fulfillment.

Lifelong Learning and Educational Pursuits

Retirement is not the end of learning; it's a new beginning. Engaging in lifelong learning keeps your mind sharp, expands your horizons, and adds richness to your retirement lifestyle.

Continuing Education Courses: Many universities and community centers offer continuing education programs where you can explore new subjects or deepen your knowledge in areas of interest.

Artistic Pursuits: If you've always wanted to learn a new instrument, dance style, or art form, retirement provides the time and opportunity to indulge in these creative passions.

Pursuing meaningful activities and engaging in volunteer opportunities during retirement can elevate your sense of purpose and fulfillment. Whether you join community clubs, offer mentorship, support charitable causes, or explore new educational pursuits, embracing a purpose-driven retirement lifestyle enriches your life and creates a positive impact on the world around you.

As you discover and nurture these meaningful connections and experiences, your retirement years will be filled with joy, personal growth, and a profound sense of fulfillment.

The Importance of Physical and Mental Well-Being in Retirement

Retirement marks a significant transition in life, offering the opportunity to focus on personal well-being and health. Prioritizing physical and mental well-being during retirement is essential for maintaining a high quality of life, staying active, and making the most of this exciting chapter. Let's delve into the various aspects of physical and mental well-being and how you can embrace a healthy and fulfilling retirement lifestyle.

Regular Exercise for a Healthy Body

Staying physically active is crucial for maintaining a healthy body and preventing age-related health issues. Regular exercise not only improves physical health but also has positive effects on mental well-being.

Tailoring Exercise to Your Needs: As you age, your exercise routine may require adjustments. Choose activities that align with your fitness level, interests, and any specific health conditions. Options like walking, swimming, yoga, or cycling offer low-impact and enjoyable ways to stay active.

Strength Training: Incorporate strength training exercises to maintain muscle mass and bone density, promoting better posture and overall strength.

Group Fitness Classes: Joining group fitness classes at local gyms or community centers can provide a social component to exercise, keeping you motivated and engaged.

Nurturing a Healthy Diet

A balanced and nutritious diet plays a central role in supporting overall health and well-being during retirement.

Nutrient-Rich Foods: Focus on a diet rich in fruits, vegetables, whole grains, lean proteins, and healthy fats. These provide essential nutrients and help maintain energy levels.

Hydration: Drink plenty of water throughout the day to stay properly hydrated, as hydration is essential for various bodily functions.

Mindful Eating: Pay attention to portion sizes and practice mindful eating, savoring each meal and avoiding overeating.

Prioritizing Mental and Emotional Well-Being

Retirement is an excellent time to focus on mental and emotional health, fostering a positive outlook and overall happiness.

Mindfulness and Meditation: Practice mindfulness and meditation to reduce stress, enhance self-awareness, and cultivate a sense of calm and contentment.

Social Connections: Stay socially connected with friends, family, and community groups. Engaging in social activities can combat feelings of isolation and loneliness.

Engaging in Intellectual Stimulation: Keep your mind sharp and engaged by pursuing intellectual activities like reading, puzzles, or learning new skills.

Regular Health Checkups and Preventive Care

Regular health checkups and preventive care are essential for staying proactive about your health during retirement.

Medical Screenings: Schedule regular medical screenings to monitor your health and detect any potential health issues early.

Vaccinations: Stay up to date with vaccinations recommended for seniors, including flu shots and other preventive measures.

Embracing a Work-Life Balance

While retirement offers the freedom to explore new activities and hobbies, it's essential to strike a balance between relaxation and engagement.

Structured Daily Routine: Establish a structured daily routine that includes time for hobbies, social activities, exercise, and relaxation.

Flexibility and Adaptability: Embrace the flexibility retirement offers, allowing you to adjust your schedule to accommodate new interests and experiences.

The importance of physical and mental well-being cannot be overstated in retirement. Prioritizing regular exercise, a balanced diet, mental stimulation, and social connections enriches your retirement lifestyle and promotes overall health and happiness.

Additionally, staying proactive about health checkups and preventive care ensures you can enjoy a fulfilling and vibrant retirement journey. By embracing a holistic approach to well-being, you can make the most of this exciting chapter and create a purposeful and enriching retirement lifestyle.

Travel and Adventure in Retirement

Retirement opens the door to new horizons and exciting adventures, including the opportunity to explore various travel destinations and create cherished memories. Planning your travel experiences and creating a budget ensures that you can embark on memorable adventures while maintaining financial security during retirement.

Creating a Travel Budget

Before jetting off to your dream destinations, it's essential to establish a well-thought-out travel budget that aligns with your financial goals and retirement income. Creating a budget provides a clear picture of your travel possibilities and helps you make informed decisions about your travel plans.

Assess Your Finances: Start by assessing your retirement savings, income sources, and any additional funds earmarked for travel. Understanding your financial situation allows you to allocate an appropriate amount to your travel budget.

Define Your Travel Goals: Consider your travel preferences and desires. Do you dream of embarking on luxury cruises, exploring exotic locations, or enjoying road trips to scenic destinations? Defining your travel goals will shape the overall budget.

Account for Travel Expenses: Account for all travel-related expenses, including flights or transportation, accommodation, meals, activities, travel insurance, and souvenirs. Factor in potential medical expenses if traveling abroad.

Emergency Fund: It's wise to set aside an emergency fund for unexpected situations that may arise during your travels. Having a safety net ensures you can enjoy your adventures without undue worry.

Planning Memorable Adventures

Once you've established your travel budget, it's time to plan memorable adventures that align with your interests and preferences. Retirement travel allows you to tailor your experiences to create cherished memories that will last a lifetime.

Bucket List Destinations: Consider visiting destinations that have been on your bucket list for years. Whether it's witnessing the northern lights, exploring ancient ruins, or sailing around the world, retirement offers the freedom to pursue your travel dreams.

Off-the-Beaten-Path Experiences: Embrace unique and off-the-beaten-path experiences that expose you to different cultures, traditions, and landscapes. Seek out local festivals, culinary delights, and immersive cultural activities.

Slow Travel: Rather than rushing from one destination to another, opt for slow travel, allowing you to savor each experience fully. Spending more time in a single location allows for a deeper connection with the culture and community.

Traveling with Loved Ones: Consider inviting family members or close friends to join you on your adventures. Shared experiences create lasting bonds and enhance the joy of exploration.

Sustainable and Responsible Travel

As a responsible traveler, be mindful of your impact on the environment and local communities. Sustainable and responsible travel practices contribute to the preservation of natural resources and cultural heritage.

Eco-Friendly Accommodation: Choose eco-friendly accommodation options that prioritize sustainability and minimize environmental impact.

Supporting Local Businesses: Contribute to the local economy by supporting small businesses, local artisans, and community initiatives.

Respect for Culture and Traditions: Embrace cultural diversity with respect and curiosity. Learn about local customs and traditions and engage with the community respectfully.

Creating a travel budget and planning memorable adventures are integral to making the most of your retirement journey. By understanding your financial capabilities and aligning your travel plans with your interests, you can embark on exciting adventures that align with your retirement goals.

Embrace responsible and sustainable travel practices to ensure that your experiences leave a positive impact on the destinations you visit. Whether you're exploring breathtaking landscapes, immersing in new cultures, or spending quality time with loved ones, retirement travel offers the chance to create cherished memories that will forever enrich your life.

International Retirement Considerations and Expat Living

Retirement is an opportune time to explore new horizons, and for some individuals, this includes the possibility of retiring abroad or becoming an expatriate. International retirement and expat living offer unique experiences, cultural immersion, and a chance to embrace a different way of life. However, before leaping, there are essential considerations and practicalities to address.

Retiring Abroad

Retiring abroad involves relocating to a different country to spend your retirement years. It offers the chance to experience diverse cultures, climates, and lifestyles. However, it requires careful planning and research to ensure a smooth transition.

Research Potential Destinations: Consider countries that align with your interests, climate preferences, and lifestyle expectations. Research aspects like cost of living, healthcare quality, safety, and cultural compatibility.

Visa and Residency: Understand the visa and residency requirements of your chosen destination. Some countries offer retirement-specific visas or residency programs for retirees.

Healthcare: Assess the quality and accessibility of healthcare services in your destination country. Determine if you need private health insurance or if your current insurance covers international healthcare.

Language and Cultural Adaptation: If the destination has a different language and culture, consider language classes and cultural adaptation strategies to ease integration.

Financial Considerations: Evaluate the financial aspects, including currency exchange rates, tax implications, and managing your finances from a foreign country.

Expat Living:

Becoming an expatriate involves living and working in a foreign country, either temporarily or permanently. Expats often relocate for employment opportunities, a change of lifestyle, or the desire to experience new cultures.

Job Opportunities: If you plan to work as an expatriate, research job prospects and understand the employment regulations and requirements in the destination country.

Housing and Cost of Living: Explore housing options, neighborhoods, and the cost of living in your chosen location. Consider renting initially to assess the suitability of the area before committing to purchasing a property.

Support Networks: Seek out expat communities, social groups, or clubs that can provide support and camaraderie during your time abroad.

Education and Family Considerations: If you have dependents or are planning to start a family, research the education system and family-friendly amenities in the destination country.

Legal and Financial Implications: Consult legal and financial advisors to understand the legalities of living abroad, tax responsibilities, and how to manage financial affairs effectively.

Personal and Cultural Enrichment

Retiring abroad or becoming an expatriate offers the opportunity for personal and cultural enrichment. Embracing a new way of life, engaging with diverse cultures, and overcoming challenges broaden your perspective and enrich your retirement experience.

Learning New Languages: Mastering a new language enhances your ability to communicate, build relationships, and fully integrate into the local community.

Embracing Cultural Traditions: Participate in local festivals, traditions, and customs, which foster mutual respect and appreciation for diverse cultures.

Exploration and Adventure: Use the opportunity to explore the destination's landmarks, historical sites, and natural wonders. Embrace the adventure and create lasting memories.

International retirement and expat living present unique opportunities for cultural immersion and personal growth during retirement. However, careful planning, research, and preparation are vital to ensure a successful and fulfilling experience.

By considering factors like visa requirements, healthcare, cost of living, job opportunities, and cultural adaptation, you can make informed decisions that align with your retirement goals. Embracing a life abroad brings adventure, enrichment, and a profound sense of discovery as you create a purposeful and meaningful retirement lifestyle in a new and exciting setting.

Chapter 8

Protecting Against Financial Frauds and Scams

As retirees embrace their golden years, financial security and protection against scams become increasingly crucial. Unfortunately, seniors are often targeted by scammers seeking to exploit their vulnerabilities and financial naivety. In this chapter, we'll explore common scams targeting seniors, ways to recognize red flags and essential strategies for safeguarding personal information and digital security.

Common Scams Targeting Seniors and How to Avoid Them

As retirees embrace their golden years, they often become the target of various scams and fraudulent schemes. Scammers prey on the trusting nature of seniors, aiming to exploit their vulnerabilities and lack of familiarity with modern technologies.

Understanding the common scams that target seniors and learning how to avoid falling victim to them is essential for safeguarding their financial security and peace of mind.

Social Security and Medicare Scams

Scammers frequently impersonate representatives from Social Security and Medicare, reaching out to seniors through phone calls, emails, or even in person. They may claim that the senior's benefits are at risk, demand immediate payment for supposed services, or ask for sensitive personal information.

Seniors must be cautious and verify any such communications. Government agencies like Social Security and Medicare rarely request personal information over the phone or through email. If in doubt, seniors should hang up and call the official agency's phone number listed on their official website.

Phishing and Email Scams

Phishing scams use deceptive emails that appear to be from legitimate sources, but they are designed to trick recipients into sharing personal information or clicking on malicious links. Seniors should exercise caution when opening emails from unknown sources or when they contain urgent requests for personal information.

Scammers often use fear tactics, pretending to be from a financial institution or a reputable company, to obtain sensitive data. To avoid falling victim to phishing scams, seniors should carefully verify the sender's email address and avoid clicking on any suspicious links.

Investment and Financial Scams

Fraudulent investment schemes targeting seniors promise high returns and low risks, enticing them to invest their retirement savings. These scams often employ persuasive language and testimonials from supposed satisfied investors.

Seniors must be wary of unsolicited investment opportunities and avoid making hasty decisions based on promises of quick wealth. Before making any financial decisions, seniors should thoroughly research the investment opportunity, consult with trusted financial advisors, and verify the legitimacy of the offering.

Sweepstakes and Lottery Scams

In this type of scam, seniors receive a notification claiming they have won a prize in a sweepstakes or lottery. However, to claim the prize, they are asked to pay fees, taxes, or other expenses upfront. Legitimate sweepstakes and lotteries do not require winners to pay to claim their prizes. Seniors should be cautious about unsolicited notifications of winning and avoid sharing any financial information or sending money to unknown entities.

Grandparent Scams

Grandparent scams target seniors by pretending to be a grandchild or another family member in distress. Scammers claim they are facing an emergency and urgently need financial assistance. The caller may even imitate the grandchild's voice, making the situation seem more believable. To avoid falling for this scam, seniors should verify the identity of the caller by asking personal questions that only their true grandchild would know. It's important not to rush into sending money without confirming the situation with other family members.

Protecting seniors from financial frauds and scams requires awareness, vigilance, and education. By understanding the common scams that target seniors and learning how to recognize red flags, they can take proactive steps to safeguard their financial well-being.

Encouraging open conversations about financial security, sharing knowledge about different scams, and seeking guidance from trusted financial advisors all play vital roles in empowering seniors to avoid falling victim to fraudulent schemes. Through informed decision-making and cautiousness, seniors can enjoy their retirement years with confidence and peace of mind.

Recognizing Red Flags and Warning Signs

As seniors enjoy their retirement years, they need to stay vigilant and informed about the various red flags and warning signs that can help them recognize potential scams. Scammers often use sophisticated tactics to exploit vulnerabilities, but by being aware and cautious, seniors can protect themselves from falling victim to fraudulent schemes.

Urgency and High-Pressure Tactics

Scammers often create a sense of urgency to pressure their targets into making quick decisions without proper consideration. They might claim that an opportunity is available for a limited time or that immediate action is required to avoid negative consequences. Seniors must be cautious when faced with high-pressure tactics and refrain from making hasty decisions. Legitimate offers and opportunities will not disappear overnight, allowing seniors to take the time to research and verify the information.

Unsolicited Contact

Be wary of unsolicited phone calls, emails, or messages that request personal information or financial transactions. Scammers may pose as representatives from reputable organizations, such as banks, government agencies, or charitable institutions. Seniors should always verify the authenticity of such communications before sharing any sensitive data or responding to requests.

Request for Gift Cards or Wire Transfers

Scammers often demand payment through unconventional methods, such as gift cards or wire transfers. These payment methods are preferred by scammers because they are difficult to trace and retrieve once the transaction is completed. Seniors should be cautious when asked to make payments using gift cards or wire transfers, especially if the request comes from an unknown or suspicious source.

Poor Grammar and Spelling

Many scam communications, including emails and messages, contain grammar and spelling errors. Scammers may not be proficient in the language they are using or may not have proper proofreading processes in place. Seniors should treat any communication with poor grammar and spelling as suspicious and avoid engaging with such messages.

Unknown Senders

Exercise caution when dealing with messages or emails from unknown senders. Scammers often use generic email addresses or disguise their identities to trick recipients into thinking they are from legitimate sources. Seniors should avoid clicking on links or downloading attachments from unknown senders, as they may contain malware or lead to phishing websites.

Pressure to Share Personal Information

Legitimate organizations rarely request sensitive personal information, such as Social Security numbers, bank account details, or passwords, over the phone or through email. Seniors should be cautious about sharing such information and only do so after verifying the legitimacy of the request and the identity of the requester.

Recognizing red flags and warning signs is a critical aspect of protecting seniors from financial fraud and scams. By staying informed about common tactics used by scammers and maintaining a healthy skepticism towards unsolicited communications, seniors can enhance their ability to detect potential scams.

Seniors need to share their experiences and discuss any suspicious encounters with family members or trusted friends. Additionally, staying updated on the latest scams and sharing information within the community can create a protective network that supports seniors in avoiding fraudulent schemes.

Through a combination of awareness, caution, and open communication, seniors can enjoy their retirement with greater confidence and financial security.

Safeguarding Personal Information and Digital Security

In today's digital age, safeguarding personal information and maintaining strong digital security is of utmost importance for seniors to protect themselves from potential scams and fraud. Scammers often exploit vulnerabilities in online platforms and use deceptive tactics to obtain sensitive data. By implementing robust security measures and following best practices, seniors can significantly reduce their risk of falling victim to digital scams.

Strong Passwords

Creating strong and unique passwords is the first line of defense against unauthorized access to online accounts. Seniors should avoid using easily guessable passwords like birthdates or common words. Instead, opt for a combination of upper and lower case letters, numbers, and special characters. Using different passwords for each online account ensures that a breach in one account doesn't compromise others.

Two-Factor Authentication

Enabling two-factor authentication (2FA) provides an additional layer of security. With 2FA, users must enter a one-time code sent to their mobile device or email to verify their identity when logging into an account. Even if someone obtains a password, they would still need access to the user's mobile device or email to complete the login process.

Avoiding Phishing Attempts

Phishing is a common tactic used by scammers to trick individuals into revealing personal information or clicking on malicious links. Seniors should be cautious of unsolicited emails, messages, or phone calls asking for sensitive data. To verify the legitimacy of an email, they can hover over hyperlinks without clicking to see the actual URL destination. Additionally, contacting the company or organization directly through official channels can help confirm the legitimacy of any requests.

Secure Wi-Fi Networks

Using secure Wi-Fi networks is vital, especially when conducting financial transactions or accessing sensitive information online. Public Wi-Fi networks are often unsecured and can be easily intercepted by hackers. Seniors should avoid accessing personal accounts or conducting financial activities on public networks and instead opt for secure, password-protected networks or use a virtual private network (VPN) for added protection.

Protecting Social Media Privacy

Seniors should be mindful of the information they share on social media platforms. Oversharing personal details or travel plans may expose them to potential scams. Scammers often use publicly available information from social media to craft targeted attacks. Adjusting privacy settings and restricting access to personal information can minimize this risk.

Regular Software Updates

Keeping software and devices up to date is crucial for maintaining strong digital security. Software updates often include important security patches that address vulnerabilities discovered by developers. Seniors should ensure that their devices, operating systems, and antivirus software are regularly updated to the latest versions.

Safeguarding personal information and maintaining strong digital security are integral aspects of protecting seniors from scams and fraud in the digital landscape. By adopting best practices such as using strong passwords, enabling two-factor authentication, avoiding phishing attempts, and protecting social media privacy, seniors can reduce their vulnerability to online threats.

Regularly updating software and staying informed about the latest digital security trends further enhances their ability to navigate the digital world safely. Empowering seniors with knowledge and promoting digital literacy will help them enjoy a secure and confident retirement experience.

Staying Informed and Prepared for Financial Security

Working with Trusted Advisors and Professionals

In the pursuit of a secure and fulfilling retirement, seniors often seek guidance and assistance from financial advisors and professionals. Collaborating with trusted experts can provide valuable insights, personalized advice, and a sense of security in managing financial affairs. However, seniors need to exercise caution and diligence when selecting and working with advisors to ensure they are partnering with reputable and reliable professionals.

Research and Credentials

When searching for financial advisors, seniors should conduct thorough research and verify their credentials. Reputable advisors will have the necessary qualifications, such as certifications, licenses, and affiliations with recognized financial organizations. Credentials like Certified Financial Planner (CFP) or Chartered Financial Analyst (CFA) demonstrate a commitment to high ethical standards and professional expertise.

Fiduciary Responsibility

Seeking advisors who have a fiduciary responsibility is crucial. Fiduciary advisors are legally obligated to act in their client's best interests, prioritizing their financial well-being over personal gain. This ensures that the advice provided aligns with the client's goals and objectives, without any conflicts of interest.

Transparent Fee Structure

Seniors should clearly understand the fee structure of the advisor's services. Reputable advisors are transparent about their fees, including any commissions or charges for their services. Hidden fees or excessive costs should raise red flags, and seniors should seek clarification before committing to any financial advice or product.

Personalized Financial Planning

Trusted advisors take the time to understand each client's unique financial situation, goals, and risk tolerance. They tailor financial plans to address specific needs and circumstances, offering personalized solutions rather than generic recommendations. Seniors should be cautious of one-size-fits-all approaches and opt for advisors who take a comprehensive view of their financial life.

Client References and Reviews

Seniors can gain insight into an advisor's reputation and track record by seeking client references or reading reviews and testimonials. Positive feedback from satisfied clients can provide reassurance, while consistent negative reviews or complaints should be taken seriously.

Avoiding High-Pressure Sales Tactics

Seniors should be wary of advisors who employ high-pressure sales tactics to promote specific financial products or investments. A reputable advisor will prioritize education and informed decision-making, rather than rushing clients into making quick and potentially ill-advised choices.

Continual Education and Communication

Trusted advisors stay informed about the latest financial trends, regulations, and strategies. They maintain open lines of communication with their clients, providing regular updates on the progress of financial plans and addressing any concerns or questions that arise.

Working with trusted advisors and professionals can significantly contribute to a senior's financial security and protection against scams. By conducting due diligence in selecting reputable advisors with fiduciary responsibility, transparent fee structures, and personalized financial planning, seniors can make informed choices aligned with their goals.

Continual education and open communication with advisors foster a collaborative and supportive relationship, enabling seniors to navigate their retirement years with confidence and peace of mind.

Developing an Emergency Fund and Contingency Plan

In the pursuit of a secure retirement, seniors need to establish an emergency fund and develop a comprehensive contingency plan. Life is unpredictable, and unexpected events such as medical emergencies, natural disasters, or economic downturns can have a significant impact on one's financial stability.

By proactively preparing for unforeseen circumstances, seniors can mitigate potential risks and safeguard their financial well-being.

The Importance of an Emergency Fund

An emergency fund is a reserve of cash set aside to cover urgent and unexpected expenses. It serves as a financial safety net, providing peace of mind and a sense of security during challenging times. The fund should ideally cover three to six months' worth of living expenses, allowing seniors to navigate through temporary disruptions without relying on credit or taking out loans.

Building an Emergency Fund

Building an emergency fund requires discipline and consistent saving habits. Seniors can start by allocating a portion of their income each month to the fund until it reaches the desired level. It's essential to keep the fund in a liquid and easily accessible account, such as a savings or money market account. While building the emergency fund, seniors should prioritize it over non-essential expenses and avoid tapping into it for non-urgent purposes.

Identifying Contingency Measures

Developing a contingency plan involves anticipating potential risks and outlining strategies to address them. Seniors should identify specific scenarios that could impact their financial stability and consider various courses of action. For example, a contingency plan might include provisions for handling medical emergencies, market downturns, or unexpected home repairs.

Evaluating Insurance Coverage

Insurance plays a critical role in a comprehensive contingency plan. Seniors should review and update their insurance coverage regularly to ensure it aligns with their current needs and life circumstances. Health insurance, long-term care insurance, homeowner's insurance, and other policies should provide adequate coverage and protection.

Establishing Power of Attorney and Advance Directives

Seniors should establish power of attorney and create advance directives to ensure that their wishes are respected and their affairs are handled according to their preferences in case of incapacitation. These legal documents appoint trusted individuals to make decisions on their behalf, ensuring their financial and medical interests are protected.

Regular Plan Review and Updates

A contingency plan should not be a one-time exercise but rather a living document that is regularly reviewed and updated as circumstances change. Seniors should periodically revisit their plans, considering changes in financial goals, health status, or family situations. Staying proactive and adaptive will strengthen the effectiveness of the contingency plan over time.

Developing an emergency fund and contingency plan is a proactive approach to safeguarding financial security during retirement. An emergency fund provides a safety net to weather unexpected expenses, while a comprehensive contingency plan anticipates potential risks and outlines strategies to address them.

By establishing a well-thought-out plan and regularly reviewing and updating it, seniors can face life's uncertainties with greater confidence and resilience. These measures, combined with other protective strategies discussed in this chapter, contribute to a comprehensive approach to protecting against financial fraud and scams, ensuring a secure and fulfilling retirement experience.

Chapter 9

Celebrating Your Fearless Retirement

Reflecting on Your Financial Journey and Achievements

As seniors embark on their retirement journey, it is essential to take a moment to reflect on the financial milestones they have achieved and the challenges they have overcome. Retirement marks the culmination of years of hard work, careful planning, and financial discipline. Taking the time to acknowledge these milestones and challenges can provide seniors with a deep sense of fulfillment and appreciation for their financial journey.

Acknowledging Milestones

Throughout their working lives, seniors have likely achieved significant financial milestones. These milestones represent key accomplishments and goals met along the way. They may include paying off student loans, purchasing a home, funding children's education, or reaching specific savings targets for retirement.

Acknowledging these milestones allows seniors to recognize the progress they have made and the positive impact of their financial decisions. It reinforces their confidence in their ability to set and achieve financial goals, providing a sense of satisfaction and empowerment.

Example:

Imagine the sense of pride and accomplishment a senior feels when they reflect on the day they made their final mortgage payment. They realize how years of diligent budgeting and disciplined saving allowed them to become a homeowner and achieve financial freedom. Celebrating this milestone reaffirms their belief in their financial abilities and motivates them to pursue new goals in retirement.

Overcoming Challenges

Financial journeys are rarely without challenges. Seniors may have faced unexpected financial setbacks, market downturns, job loss, or other difficulties throughout their careers. Overcoming these challenges demonstrates resilience and adaptability in the face of adversity.

By acknowledging the challenges, they have overcome, seniors gain a deeper understanding of their financial strengths and the strategies that served them well during difficult times. It also offers valuable insights into the importance of financial preparedness and contingency planning.

Example:

A senior reflects on a time when they experienced a sudden medical emergency that resulted in significant medical bills. However, thanks to their emergency fund and health insurance coverage, they were able to manage the expenses without derailing their long-term financial plans. Recognizing their ability to handle such a challenging situation reinforces the importance of maintaining emergency funds and adequate insurance coverage in retirement.

The Power of Resilience and Adaptability

Acknowledging both milestones and challenges underscores the senior's resilience and adaptability throughout their financial journey. By navigating the highs and lows of their financial life, seniors have honed their ability to adjust to changing circumstances and make informed decisions.

Resilience empowers seniors to face the uncertainties of retirement with confidence, knowing that they have successfully weathered storms in the past. It provides a strong foundation for embracing new opportunities and pursuing fulfilling experiences in retirement.

Example:

A senior reflects on a career change they made later in life, which initially presented financial challenges but ultimately led to greater job satisfaction and a more substantial income. The ability to adapt to a changing job market and take proactive steps to enhance their skills empowered them to build a more secure financial future.

This chapter encourages seniors to take time to reflect on their financial journey, acknowledging both their milestones and the challenges they have faced. Celebrating their achievements and recognizing their ability to overcome adversity can bring a deep sense of satisfaction and gratitude in retirement.

It reinforces the value of disciplined financial planning and serves as a reminder that with thoughtful preparation and determination, seniors can confidently navigate the path to a fearless and fulfilling retirement.

Resilience and adaptability are powerful attributes that contribute to a successful retirement, allowing seniors to embrace new opportunities and create a meaningful and purposeful post-career life.

Embracing a Positive and Grateful Attitude toward Retirement

As seniors transition into retirement, cultivating a positive and grateful attitude can profoundly impact their overall well-being and experience during this new phase of life. Retirement represents an opportunity to shift focus from the stresses of work and financial responsibilities to a time of leisure, personal growth, and exploration.

The Power of Gratitude

Expressing gratitude for the resources and opportunities that retirement offers can bring a profound sense of contentment and fulfillment. It is a time to reflect on the hard work and efforts put into achieving financial security and the freedom it now provides.

Gratitude allows seniors to find joy in the simple pleasures of life and develop a positive outlook on their retirement years.

Gratefulness can be practiced in various ways, such as keeping a gratitude journal, sharing appreciation with loved ones, or taking time to enjoy and be present in everyday moments. By embracing gratitude, seniors can experience greater happiness and a deeper sense of connection to the people and experiences that matter most to them.

Example:

A retired couple spends their mornings sipping coffee on their porch, watching the sunrise together. They express gratitude for the tranquility of retirement and the opportunity to enjoy peaceful moments in each other's company. This daily practice of gratitude not only enhances their overall well-being but also strengthens their emotional bond, as they appreciate the time they can now spend together without the rush of work.

Finding Fulfillment in New Pursuits

Retirement offers the chance to explore passions, interests, and hobbies that may have been set aside during the demands of a career. Embracing new pursuits and lifelong dreams can lead to a sense of purpose and excitement in retirement.

Many retirees discover that engaging in activities they are passionate about brings a renewed sense of fulfillment and happiness. Whether it's volunteering for a cause they believe in, taking up a creative hobby, or learning a new skill, these activities can provide a sense of purpose and fulfillment beyond their working years.

Example:

A retiree always had a love for animals but couldn't devote much time to it while working. In retirement, they volunteer at a local animal shelter, where their compassion and dedication make a positive impact on the lives of rescued animals. This newfound purpose brings them immense satisfaction and a sense of making a difference, reaffirming the idea that retirement is a time to pursue passions and contribute to causes that are meaningful to them.

Embracing Change and Growth

Retirement often involves significant life changes, including shifts in daily routines, social interactions, and personal identity. Embracing these changes and viewing them as opportunities for growth can lead to a more fulfilling retirement experience.

Seniors can approach retirement with an open mind, embracing the chance to explore new interests, cultivate meaningful relationships, and evolve as individuals. This attitude fosters adaptability and resilience in the face of change, allowing retirees to confidently navigate the transition to post-career life.

Example:

Retiree finds themselves initially uncertain about how to structure their days in retirement, missing the routine of their former job. However, they gradually embrace the freedom retirement provides, using their time to pursue hobbies, attend classes, and connect with like-minded individuals in community groups. This openness to change and willingness to explore new possibilities enriches their retirement journey, making it a time of growth and self-discovery.

We encourage seniors to celebrate their financial journey and achievements with a sense of contentment and appreciation, making the most of this exciting phase of life. By embracing change and personal growth, retirees can embark on a meaningful post-career life filled with purpose, joy, and the sense of living their best years yet.

Sharing Your Knowledge and Legacy with Others

After accumulating a lifetime of experiences and wisdom, seniors have the opportunity to share their knowledge and leave a lasting legacy for future generations. Actively engaging in this process can bring fulfillment and a sense of purpose in retirement.

Mentoring Future Retirees and Younger Generations

Retirement is not just a time of personal fulfillment; it is also an opportunity to pass on wisdom and knowledge to future retirees and younger generations. Seniors who have experienced the challenges and triumphs of retirement are uniquely positioned to offer valuable insights and guidance to those who are on the cusp of embarking on their retirement journeys.

Sharing Life Lessons and Experiences

Mentoring allows retirees to share their life lessons and experiences, offering practical advice and emotional support to those who are about to enter the retirement phase. Whether it's family members, friends, or colleagues, providing guidance based on personal experiences can be immensely valuable to those seeking reassurance and direction.

Seniors can discuss the importance of financial planning, the significance of maintaining a positive outlook, and the rewards of pursuing fulfilling activities in retirement. By imparting their knowledge, retirees can empower others to approach retirement with confidence and a sense of preparedness.

Example:

Retiree mentors their adult children who are planning for their retirement. They share the importance of starting to save early, making strategic investment decisions, and managing debt responsibly. The adult children benefit from their parents' insights and gain a deeper understanding of the steps needed to achieve financial security in retirement.

Offering Emotional Support

Transitioning into retirement can be emotionally challenging, as it often involves leaving behind a familiar work environment and adjusting to a new lifestyle. Seniors who have successfully navigated this transition can provide much-needed emotional support to those who are about to undergo a similar experience.

By empathizing with the concerns and anxieties of future retirees, mentors can offer reassurance and understanding. They can share how they coped with the emotional aspects of retirement and the strategies they used to find purpose and fulfillment in their post-career life.

Example:

A retiree volunteers as a mentor in a retirement community, providing emotional support to new residents who have recently retired. They organize group discussions and one-on-one sessions, encouraging open dialogue about the challenges and joys of retirement. Their empathetic approach and willingness to listen create a sense of camaraderie among the retirees, fostering a supportive and caring community.

Fostering Intergenerational Connections

Mentoring offers an opportunity for intergenerational connections, bridging the gap between older and younger individuals. Retirees who engage in mentoring relationships can build meaningful connections with younger generations, sharing perspectives and learning from each other.

By connecting with younger individuals, retirees gain fresh insights into current trends, technology, and societal changes. At the same time, younger mentees benefit from the wisdom and life experience of their mentors, gaining valuable knowledge that can shape their own future decisions.

Example:

A retiree volunteers as a mentor at a local community center, where they engage with young adults who are preparing to enter the workforce. Through discussions and workshops, they share their experiences about work-life balance, setting career goals, and the importance of maintaining financial stability.

In return, they learn about emerging career paths and new technologies, fostering an enriching and mutually beneficial relationship.

Mentoring future retirees and younger generations is a rewarding aspect of celebrating a fearless retirement. By sharing life lessons, offering emotional support, and fostering intergenerational connections, retirees contribute to the well-being and success of others as they embark on their retirement journeys.

This chapter encourages retirees to embrace mentoring opportunities, as it allows them to leave a lasting legacy by empowering others with the knowledge and wisdom gained throughout their own retirement experiences.

Through mentoring, retirees can make a meaningful impact on the lives of future generations, leaving a positive and enduring influence on their communities and beyond.

Leaving a Lasting Impact on Your Community and Beyond

Retirement presents a unique opportunity for seniors to leave a lasting impact on their community and beyond. Having worked hard throughout their careers and accumulated a wealth of knowledge and experience, retirees now have the chance to give back, make a difference, and leave a positive legacy for future generations.

Community Involvement and Volunteerism

One of the most fulfilling ways retirees can leave an impact is through community involvement and volunteer work. By dedicating their time and skills to local organizations, charities, and causes they care about, retirees can contribute to the well-being of their communities.

Volunteer work allows retirees to apply their expertise and passions in meaningful ways. Whether it's mentoring local youth, supporting underprivileged individuals, or participating in environmental initiatives, retirees can use their life experiences to bring about positive change.

Example:

A retiree, with a background in finance, volunteers to provide free financial planning workshops for low-income families in their community. By sharing their knowledge of budgeting, saving, and investment, they empower families to achieve financial stability and build a better future for themselves.

Philanthropy and Charitable Giving

Retirement often provides retirees with the financial means to engage in philanthropy and charitable giving. They can support causes they are passionate about by making monetary donations to reputable organizations.

By carefully researching and selecting organizations aligned with their values, retirees can ensure their contributions have a meaningful and sustainable impact. Whether it's supporting education, healthcare, environmental conservation, or humanitarian efforts, charitable giving allows retirees to create positive change on a broader scale.

Example:

Retiree donates a significant portion of their retirement savings to a local foundation dedicated to empowering disadvantaged youth through education and mentorship programs. Their generous contribution provides resources for the foundation to expand its initiatives, making a profound impact on the lives of countless young individuals.

Environmental Stewardship

Retirees can embrace environmental stewardship and advocate for sustainable practices in their communities. This may involve participating in local conservation efforts, promoting recycling and waste reduction, or supporting initiatives that combat climate change.

By being role models for eco-friendly living, retirees can inspire others to adopt more sustainable habits, creating a ripple effect of positive change for the environment.

A retiree takes the lead in organizing a neighborhood clean-up initiative, encouraging fellow residents to come together and beautify their surroundings. Their efforts inspire others to take pride in their community and actively participate in environmental preservation.

Sharing Knowledge and Experiences

Beyond their immediate community, retirees can leave a lasting impact by sharing their knowledge and experiences with a broader audience. This can be achieved through writing, public speaking engagements, or online platforms.

By documenting their life journey, including the challenges they've faced and the lessons they've learned, retirees can inspire and guide others on their paths to success and fulfillment.

For example; a retiree writes a memoir detailing their career journey, financial triumphs, and personal growth. Their book becomes a source of inspiration for young professionals, encouraging them to pursue their passions and embrace the opportunities that life presents.

Through community involvement, volunteerism, philanthropy, environmental stewardship, and sharing knowledge, retirees can make a positive difference in the lives of others.

As they celebrate their fearless retirement, retirees have the chance to create a legacy that extends far beyond their years, leaving a lasting imprint on the world and inspiring others to lead purposeful and impactful lives.

Chapter 10

Conclusion

Embracing the Fearless Retirement Journey: Putting Your Plan into Action

As we conclude this comprehensive guide on retirement planning for those aged 50 and above, we stand at the threshold of a new and exciting chapter in life. Throughout this book, we have explored every aspect of preparing for retirement, from assessing your financial readiness to generating passive income streams and everything in between.

Now, armed with knowledge, insights, and a well-crafted plan, you are ready to embark on your fearless retirement journey.

Retirement is not merely a destination; it is a transformative journey of self-discovery, exploration, and fulfillment. It is a time to savor the rewards of a lifetime of hard work and dedication and to celebrate the freedom that comes with a secure financial future.

Armed with the wisdom gained from years of experience, you have the power to create a retirement that is tailored to your dreams and aspirations.

Celebrating the Freedom of a Secure Financial Future

One of the most empowering aspects of a well-planned retirement is the freedom it provides. No longer bound by the constraints of a nine-to-five routine or financial worries, you have the liberty to embrace life on your terms. Whether you choose to travel the world, pursue a passion project, engage in community service, or spend cherished moments with loved ones, the possibilities are limitless.

Your journey in retirement is not solitary; it is part of a larger narrative of building a legacy that extends beyond your years. As you celebrate your fearless retirement, remember the importance of sharing your knowledge, experiences, and resources with future generations.

Through mentoring, philanthropy, and environmental stewardship, you can leave a lasting impact that inspires and empowers others to follow in your footsteps.

Putting Your Plan into Action

As you move forward into retirement, take the time to revisit your comprehensive retirement plan. Take deliberate steps to put your plan into action, making adjustments along the way as needed. Stay committed to regularly assessing and rebalancing your financial strategies to align with your evolving goals and circumstances.

Embrace the challenges and opportunities that come your way with an open mind and a positive attitude. Your fearless retirement journey may present unforeseen twists and turns, but with the foundation you have built, you are well-equipped to adapt and thrive.

Remember that retirement is not a solitary endeavor; seek the support of trusted advisors, friends, and family to navigate through any uncertainties. Surround yourself with a community of like-minded individuals who share your enthusiasm for this new phase of life.

Now is the time to step boldly into the future you have envisioned. Celebrate your retirement with a sense of gratitude, purpose, and determination. Embrace the financial security you have diligently built, and relish in the countless possibilities that lie ahead.

Your fearless retirement journey has the potential to be the most rewarding and fulfilling chapter of your life. As you make memories, pursue passions, and leave a lasting legacy, may you find joy, contentment, and a profound sense of accomplishment in this new adventure.

Congratulations on taking this transformative step into your fearless retirement. Embrace it with courage, curiosity, and a heart filled with hope. This is your time to shine, and the best is yet to come.